FOUR CENTURIES OF SOUTHERN INDIANS

Four Centuries of Southern Indians

CHARLES M. HUDSON

editor

The University of Georgia Press
Athens

Library of Congress Catalog Card Number: 73–85028
ISBN: 0–8203–0332–1 (cloth); 0–8203–0362–3 (paper)

The University of Georgia Press, Athens 30602

Printed in the United States of America

Contents

Acknowledgments

All of the papers in this volume were originally presented at the nineteenth annual meeting of the American Society for Ethnohistory held in Athens, Georgia, 13–16 October 1971. I am grateful to the Institute for Behavioral Research at the University of Georgia for providing me with support and facilities while I did final editing.

CHARLES M. HUDSON

Danielsville, Georgia

Introduction

Charles M. Hudson

It is shocking to contemplate that the native people of the
southern United States have been a part of our history for over
four centuries, and yet for all the pages that have been written
about them, they remain to us as strangers, or even worse, as
caricatures. Our ignorance is especially unfortunate because at
least some of the southern or southeastern Indians possessed
what may have been the most highly centralized and complex
social structures of all the aboriginal people in North America.
John R. Swanton conservatively estimates that the southern
Indians numbered about 170,000 in 1650; more recently, however, Henry Dobyns has placed their number just before European contact at perhaps ten times Swanton's figure.[1] Whatever
their precise number, it can safely be said that compared to
Indians in other parts of North America, they were relatively
populous. In early historic times the southern Indians were
organized into large centralized chiefdoms, and in the late prehistoric period there are suggestions that they may have actually had among them one or more small incipient states.
They built large villages with monumental mounds and earth-
works; they enjoyed rich religious and artistic achievements;
and they maintained a flourishing economy based on agriculture and complemented by time-honored hunting and gathering techniques. They fought the invading Europeans for three
centuries before they were finally crushed and forced to mi-
grate west of the Mississippi River.

Who, then, were the southern Indians? In historic times they were the Catawbas and the Tuscaroras of the Carolina back-country, the Cherokees of the Appalachian Mountains and northern Georgia, the Creeks of Georgia and Alabama (some of whom fled to Florida where they became known as Seminoles), the Choctaws and Chickasaws of Mississippi and Louisiana, the Caddos of Louisiana and Texas, and several smaller and less well-known groups. But many if not all of these social entities—variously called *tribes* or *confederacies*—were relatively late developments; often they consisted of culturally and socially heterogeneous people who were driven together for survival in the face of a common white enemy. Later the Cherokees, Chickasaws, Choctaws, Creeks, and Seminoles were called *civilized tribes*, not in recognition of their aboriginal achievements, but because they successfully adopted many of the cutural patterns and social institutions of the white man.

The Indians who were found by the first Europeans in the Southeast stood at the end of many thousands of years of human experience. From the picture of southeastern prehistory which has been pieced together bit by bit by archaeologists, we see that some of the cultural patterns which made up the southeastern way of life had an antiquity in excess of six thousand years, originating in the period of cultural development that archaeologists refer to as "Archaic." But the more specific elements of the cultures observed by the earliest Europeans were products of the Mississippian culture, a way of life that first took shape in the Southeast around A.D. 500–600 and endured into the historic period. This Mississippian culture is marked by the appearance of a fully developed agriculture, the construction of large truncated mounds with public buildings on top, the existence of large population centers, and the development of a distinctive art style.[2] Some of the named groups contacted by De Soto—such as the Mocoso, Aute, Cofitachequi, Mabila, Quizquiz, and Quigualtam, to name just a few—seem to have been fully representative of the Mississippian culture. Other named groups, such as the Guale, Timucua, and Calusa of early Spanish Florida and lower Georgia, seem to have lain either on the margins of Mississippian culture or else altogether outside it. We will never know much about these groups because all of these names and many others quickly disappear from the historic record as the Indians were destroyed by new epidemic diseases and European military actions.

The true extent of the aboriginal social and cultural diversity of the southern Indians will never be known. We do know that with the exception of the Northwest Pacific Coast and California the diversity of languages in the Southeast was greater than for any other part of North America. The Southeast contained no less than four language families: Algonkian (e.g., Powhatan, Shawnee), Iroquoian (e.g., Cherokee, Tuscarora), Siouan (e.g., Tutelo, Biloxi, Catawba), and Muskogean (e.g., Choctaw-Chickasaw, Alabama, Creek). The languages which belonged to these families were as different from each other as English is from Chinese. Several other languages —including Yuchi, Natchez, Tunica, Chitimacha, Atakapa, and Timucuan—were probably distantly related to these four families, and still other languages, known only by the most fragmentary evidence, were perhaps related to still other language families.[3] It should not be assumed, however, that linguistic diversity is a reliable index of cultural diversity. James Adair, the best authority that we have on the southern Indians in the eighteenth century, states time and time again that, except for language, the southern Indians shared more cultural similarities than differences.[4] Of course, many Indians had been annihilated by this time, and perhaps many cultures, particularly the smaller more fragile ones, had already vanished.

But even the Indians in the historic period for whom we have relatively full documentation—the Cherokees, Choctaws, and Chickasaws, for example—do not have the place in our history that they deserve. They are so much the victims of social biases, stereotypes, and prejudices in our history and anthropology that we have a virtual amnesia about the parts of our past in which they are involved. The southern Indians have suffered more in this respect than have other Indians, and both anthropologists and historians must share the blame. Paradoxically, the anthropologists have spent great effort studying the Indians in the distant prehistoric past and the

Indians in the present or the recent past, while more or less ignoring the Indians that came in between. It is as if anthropologists give us the first and third acts, but no second act.[5] This peculiar emphasis is partly the product of the positivistic bent of anthropology and its emphasis on "observation." The Indians of the distant past are in the objects of study of the archaeologists, who find their historical evidence hidden in the earth in the form of both consciously fashioned artifacts and unconscious material by-products of human behavior. The social anthropologists, on the other hand, have emphasized firsthand field research with living people. Here also the emphasis is on "observation" and the use of nondocumentary materials.

In contrast, the historians are most interested in the Indians who came in between prehistory and modern times. Although it would seem that their research would fill in precisely the gap left by the anthropologists, we find that this is not the case. Although historians have covered the needed time period, they have consistently written Indian history from a white point of view, and they have done so even when consciously trying to write from an Indian point of view. For the historian, Indian history is almost always the history of relations between the Indian and the white man. Thus, anthropologists and historians do not complement each other's work as they should, and even the young field of ethnohistory has not brought about the rapprochement which many had hoped for.[6] Indeed, the anthropologists call the Cherokees and Creeks *southeastern* Indians, emphasizing the fact that their ancestral home was in the southeastern culture area, which differed in specific cultural ways from adjacent culture areas, while the historians call them *southern* Indians, emphasizing their role in white southern history.

But if historians and anthropologists have their weaknesses, they also have their strengths. The historian is skilled at locating and working with documentary materials, at sifting masses of complex evidence critically, and at writing reliable accounts of what has taken place through time. Lacking the anthropologist's positivistic bias, the historian is far more likely to question existing interpretations of the past and to be skeptical about the polysyllabic concepts and high-sounding theories of the anthropologists. Historians, as Robert Berkhofer observes, know to "beware of the anthropologists bearing conclusions."[7] On the other hand, the strength of the anthropologist lies not only in his ability to wrest history from nondocumentary materials—material remains, oral history, and so on—but also in his readiness to grasp exotic points of view. Through having firsthand experience with life in other societies, as both participant and observer, and thereby coming to see reality as people in other cultures see it, the anthropologist is able to realize more fully that the "same" historical experience can be refracted into rather different versions, given different basic cultural categories and assumptions.[8] Moreover, the social anthropologist is often able to show that seemingly alien beliefs —as, for example, the belief in witchcraft and sorcery—are not as alien as they at first appear and in fact fit the facts of life in small societies remarkably well. When it is done well, social anthropology stretches our minds, making us receptive to other ways of ordering experience.

The essays in this volume are almost equally divided between anthropologists and historians, and we can clearly see in them the strengths of the two fields. From James Covington's paper we get a picture of the Timucuan Indians of the middle sixteenth century and of their uncertain relations with the French and the Spanish. In some ways these Timucuans were quite different from the southern Indians of later times, but their entanglements in French and Spanish colonial rivalry was a precursor of things to come. In Covington's paper we also gain some insight into the difficulty of establishing colonies in the Southeast. Not only were the Europeans unable at first to produce enough food to keep themselves alive, but they also had to contend with the fact that they could not dominate the southeastern Indians from the top, as the Spanish had done so effectively in the high civilizations in Latin America. In a sense, the southeastern Indians had no top, at least not in the sense that the Aztecs and Incas did. Thus, the "anarchy" which existed among these chiefdoms and made it impossible for them to cooperate effectively and resist the Europeans also made it impossible for the Europeans to rule them in any effective way.

After the establishment of the English colonies, the trade in deerskins, first from Virginia and later from South Carolina, came to dominate the lives of the southern Indians. Relatively little can be understood about the southern Indians in the colonial era without taking the deerskin trade into account. Reexamining the early history of the Tuscarora Indians in this light, Douglas Boyce presents evidence that the Tuscarora were not a confederacy with two factions, as earlier authorities have argued, but were rather a collection of autonomous villages who in the early eighteenth century formed two loose alliances, divided mainly on the basis of a differential access to European trade goods. The experience of the Tuscaroras offers a clear example of the changes and problems that arose when the southern Indians found themselves dependent on European trade goods.

As the eighteenth century progressed, the southern Indians were increasingly encroached upon by the whites, who now wanted more and more land. Pushed on all sides by the frontiersmen, the Indians became increasingly desperate, and when the War for Independence came, they generally sided with the Loyalists. The American colonists' retaliation was terrible, particularly against the Cherokees. After the war was over, the Americans regarded the southern Indians as defeated allies of the British, and they determined that they should suffer accordingly. Had the Indians not found allies in the Spanish, who needed them to help check American expansion into territories claimed by Spain, they would have probably been forced to abandon their homeland long before they eventually were.

Removal is a gentle word for one of the harshest, ugliest acts in American history. In the best spirit of critical scholarship, we see in Arthur DeRosier's paper that most of our existing accounts of how the southern Indians were removed are at variance with the facts. Removal did not come about through white men and Indians sitting down at a bargaining table and subsequently honoring their commitments as gentlemen: the Indians were pressured, tricked, swindled, bullied, and, if all else failed, murdered by "land-hungry" frontiersmen. And we cannot explain the horrors of removal as the evil acts of monstrous soldiers, missionaries, and Indian agents: they were human beings just as the Indians were human beings. The responsibility lay higher.

Even though the policy of removal was pursued with great determination, the southeastern Indians were not completely eliminated from the Southeast. Small enclaves managed to remain in isolated, inaccessible areas. In some cases they became genetically mixed with other races and lost all vestiges of their aboriginal culture.[9] In other cases, as John Peterson shows in his paper, they hung on by filling up small, precarious, and often peculiar economic niches, and they retained some of their aboriginal culture.

The most characteristic work of the social anthropologist is to give us a view of an exotic culture from the inside. The problem is not so much in grasping another culture's view of reality—though this is difficult enough—but to put this reality, once grasped, into terms understandable to people in our own culture. Raymond Fogelson deals in this volume with the belief held by Cherokees (and other southeastern Indians) that there existed in this world witches and sorcerers (or conjurers). They believed that witches and sorcerers were individuals of both sexes who could affect the health, fortune, and well-being of other individuals through mystical means.

How, we ask ourselves, could the Cherokees, who went about so many things in such a rational manner, possibly hold such outlandish beliefs? A completely adequate demonstration that if one accepts certain assumptions, then Cherokee beliefs about witchcraft and sorcery are a perfectly reasonable belief system would require many hundreds of pages, as for example in E. E. Evans-Pritchard's 544-page *Witchcraft, Oracles and Magic among the Azande*. But a few crucial observations can be made in the interest of perspective. The most important thing to realize is that witchcraft, as a belief system, fits the facts of life in preliterate societies very well. In such a society, a person generally lives out his entire life in the small community. In such a community it is normal for everyone to scrutinize closely the behavior of everyone else, and people typically manage their social relationships carefully to prevent jealousy and envy on the part of others. Relationships are more intense than any in our experience, and a troubled relationship can affect many areas of a person's life. We find, therefore, that in preliterate societies, people *do* affect each other in complex ways, and witchcraft is a kind of ideological objectification of this.

Amazingly, as Albert L. Wahrhaftig's paper shows, traditional Cherokees in Oklahoma even today retain vestiges of this pattern of carefully maintained relationships, and they still resort to conjuring when ordinary social means break down. More importantly, Wahrhaftig's paper shows us how these "conservative" Cherokees cope with social change by introducing innovations for the purpose of protecting their old way of life. This, in turn, suggests that we reexamine the historic record, asking whether all those remarkable Cherokee achievements in the early nineteenth century truly came from resident whites and mixed-bloods as has heretofore been asserted.

The last essay in this volume deals, appropriately, with racism. The three races—red, white, and black—were in sustained contact for a longer period of time in the South than in any other part of North America. And although racism, the ideological reflex of this historical experience, was not invented in the South, we cannot understand any part of southern history without taking it into account. Indeed, the possibility of writing a new history of the southern Indians, and along with it a new history of the South, will depend upon our coming to grips with racism and the social conditions that produced it.

The technical problems in writing newer, more adequate accounts of the southern Indians are formidable, and the best work will eventually be done by scholars who possess both the historian's research techniques and knowledge of the past and the anthropologist's ability to see the world through the eyes of preliterate people. The standards for American Indian studies should be as high as they are for scholarly work on the people of any other part of the world. Perhaps we should require that scholars who wish to do meaningful research on American Indians acquire a working knowledge of the native languages. No historian of Greece or China would think of doing serious research without having a command of Greek or Chinese. Why, then, should a historian doing research on Cherokees or Choctaws do so without first taking the trouble to study the Cherokee or Choctaw language? It would perhaps be unnecessary—though it would certainly be desirable—to ask the scholar to acquire a conversational command of the language, but even a few months of work at learning Cherokee or Choctaw would be enough to dispel the stereotype of the simple-minded Indian and to bring about the realization that the speakers of these languages might see things differently from the way we see them. Moreover, I share the hope of many of my colleagues that more and more of the scholarship on American Indians will be done by scholars who are themselves Indian.[10] Here at last we should get history from an Indian point of view.[11]

NOTES

1. John R. Swanton, *The Indians of the Southeastern United States,* Smithsonian Institution, Bureau of American Ethnology Bulletin No. 137 (Washington, D.C., 1946), pp. 11–12; Henry F. Dobyns, "An Appraisal of Techniques with a New Hemisphere Estimate," *Current Anthropology* 7 (1966): 395–416.

2. Jesse D. Jennings, *Prehistory of North America* (New York: McGraw-Hill, 1968), pp. 214–229.

3. Mary R. Haas, "Southeastern Indian Linguistics," in *Red, White and Black: Symposium on Indians in the Old South,* ed. Charles Hudson (Athens: University of Georgia Press, 1971), pp. 44–54.

4. James Adair, *History of the American Indians* (London, 1775; reprint ed., New York: Johnson Reprint, 1968).

5. The exceptions are James Mooney and John Swanton, who wrote at a time when little was known about the archaeology of the southern Indians.

6. Robert F. Berkhofer, Jr., "The Political Context of a New Indian History," *Pacific Historical Review* 40 (1971): 357–382.

7. Ibid., p. 376.

8. Charles M. Hudson, "The Historical Approach in Anthropology," in *Handbook of Social and Cultural Anthropology,* ed. John J. Honigmann (Chicago: Rand-McNally, 1974), pp. 133–136.

9. Brewton Berry, *Almost White* (New York: Macmillan, 1963) ; W. Mc-Kee Evans, *To Die Game: The Story of the Lowry Band, Indian Guerillas of Reconstruction* (Baton Rouge: Louisiana State University Press, 1971) ; William Lynwood Montell, *The Saga of Coe Ridge: A Study of Oral History* (Knoxville: University of Tennessee Press, 1970) .

10. Wilcomb Washburn, "The Writing of American Indian History: A Status Report," *Pacific Historical Review* 40 (1971) : 261–281; Jeannette Henry, "The American Indian in American History," in *Indian Voices: The First Convocation of American Indian Scholars* (San Francisco: Indian Historian Press, 1970) , pp. 105–117.

11. One purpose of the American Indian Historical Society, now publishing both *The Indian Historian* and a monograph series, is to encourage Indian scholars.

SOURCES CITED

Adair, James. *The History of the American Indians.* 1775. Reprint. New York: Johnson Reprint, 1968.

Berkhofer, Robert F., Jr. "The Political Context of a New Indian History." *Pacific Historical Review* 40 (1971) : 357–382.

Berry, Brewton. *Almost White.* New York: Macmillan, 1963.

Dobyns, Henry F. "An Appraisal of Techniques with a New Hemisphere Estimate." *Current Anthropology* 7 (1966) : 395–416.

Evans, W. McKee. *To Die Game: The Story of the Lowry Band, Indian Guerillas of Reconstruction.* Baton Rouge: Louisiana State University Press, 1971.

Haas, Mary R. "Southeastern Indian Linguistics." In *Red, White, and Black: Symposium on Indians in the Old South,* edited by Charles Hudson. Athens: University of Georgia Press, 1971.

Henry, Jeannette. "The American Indian in American History." In *Indian Voices: The First Convocation of Indian Scholars.* San Francisco: Indian Historian Press, 1970.

Hudson, Charles M. "The Historical Approach in Anthropology." In *Handbook of Social and Cultural Anthropology,* edited by John J. Honigmann. Chicago: Rand-McNally, 1974.

Jennings, Jesse D. *Prehistory of North America.* New York: McGraw-Hill, 1968.

Montell, William Lynwood. *The Saga of Coe Ridge: A Study of Oral History.* Knoxville: University of Tennessee Press, 1970.

Swanton, John R. *The Indians of the Southeastern United States.* Smithsonian Institution, Bureau of American Ethnology Bulletin no. 137. Washington, D.C., 1946.

Washburn, Wilcomb. "The Writing of American Indian History: A Status Report." *Pacific Historical Review* 40 (1971) : 261–281.

Relations between the Eastern Timucuan Indians and the French and Spanish 1564-1567

James W. Covington

The typical North American Indian tribe, lacking a strong central authority, was composed of many small towns or bands each ruled by a minor leader. Sometimes these bands or towns formed confederations and were ruled by a leader who had more power. Although the Creek confederacy included some fifty towns, the confederacy rarely united in a common cause against an enemy and, as late as the eighteenth century, held council at irregular intervals with decisions made at the councils not considered to be binding by all towns.[1] Such lack of a common cause and a strong central government made the Indian tribes extremely vulnerable to the Europeans, who were able to play one band against another and one tribe against another.

One of the first tribes to feel the effects of European intrigues was the Timucuan Indians. The people known as Timucuans lived in a general area extending from Cumberland Island and the adjacent Georgia mainland southward into Florida to Cape Canaveral, thence southwestward to Tampa Bay, and, in the northwest, to the Aucilla River.[2] A tentative grouping of the various political units and dialects of the Timucuan language would include three divisions: the eastern division, including southeastern Georgia and coastal Florida to Mosquito Inlet, and inland along the Saint John's River; the western division, bounded by a point north of present-day Ocala to the Okeefenokee Swamp and westward to the Aucilla River;[3] and the southern division, including present-day Ocala southwestward to the Tampa Bay area.[4]

This study is concerned with the eastern division of the tribe whose domain was one of the battlegrounds between the two European powers, France and Spain. The Eastern Timucuans included such confederations of towns as the Potanou, who lived in present-day Alachua County; the Saturiba, who were centered about Cumberland Island and the mouth and early reaches of the Saint John's River; the Utina, who controlled the area between the Suwannee and Saint John's Rivers; and the Fresh Water Indians, who resided southward along the middle stretches of the Saint John's River. Each of the small villages was ruled by a leader or *cacique,* but since a single village actually had little strength, the villages banded themselves together in a confederacy dominated by a major town.[5] The dominance and power of each village and confederacy depended upon its ability to wage battle and survive during an eternal state of warfare. Altogether, there may have been between five thousand and eight thousand persons in the group known as Eastern Timucuans.[6]

Evidence concerning the way of life of the Timucuans comes from two sources: the findings made by recent archaeologists and accounts written by the French and Spanish explorers and settlers who visited and lived in Florida during the sixteenth century. According to John R. Swanton, the outstanding chronicler of the southeastern Indians, the Spanish sources were scarcely adequate in some cases, and woefully deficient in most cases, but in contrast, the French during their brief stay exhibited a most lively interest in the Indians.[7] One outstanding contribution was made by the French artist Jacques Le Moyne de Morgues who sketched forty-three drawings depicting the Indian and French activities and wrote fifteen pages of description as background for the illustrations. Theodore De Bry made engravings on copper plates from the Le Moyne drawings and published them in 1591.[8]

Although the Timucuans depended upon wild game as an essential part of their diet, they cultivated maize, beans, and squash in fields situated near their villages. In addition, their diet was supplemented by persimmons, berries, roots, nuts, and other items obtained from the nearby forests, and freshwater and saltwater fish, oysters, and clams taken from the coastal waters. In November and December after the men using hoes made of fish bones attached to wooden handles cleared the fields of weeds and prepared the soil, the women dropped corn or bean seeds into small holes prepared in the soil. After planting the crops the entire town migrated inland to a site where the inhabitants sustained themselves from December to March upon acorn meal and bread, fish, turtles, bears, bison, rabbits, turkeys, deer, and other wild life. During this retreat in the woods, the Indians lived in houses which were constructed of palm or palmetto leaves and branches. It was their usual custom to dry meat and fish over a fire. These items plus corn and beans were placed in a storehouse located in a cool spot on the sandy banks of a stream or near a hill for use during the winter months.

The town in which the Indians lived for nine months of the year reflected the warlike nature of their life. The place was surrounded by a circular palisade constructed of thick logs at least twelve feet in height; in front of the palisade stood a water-filled ditch which served as a first line of defense. Situated within the confines of the wooden walls were some thirty or forty beehive-shaped family dwelling units and the much larger rectangular chief's house.[9] The principal leader's residence (or "great house") situated in the center of the village was large enough to shelter as many as one hundred persons. This large structure, constructed of logs, a palmetto leaf roof and a subterranean floor, contained sleeping accommodations arranged along the sides for many persons, a central fireplace, and a separate room for the leader and his wife.[10]

Evidence is not clear on when the first contacts took place between the Europeans and the Timucuans, but probably slave hunters from Cuba and Santo Domingo preceded Ponce de Leon to the peninsula. It was obvious from the fierce resistance he encountered that other Spaniards had come to Florida and had mistreated the natives. After Ponce de Leon's small fleet had touched Florida near the mouth of the Saint John's River, it moved some distance to the north and thence southward along the Florida coast. Since some Indians standing on the shore appeared to be friendly, Ponce came ashore to greet them, but as soon as he had landed, the natives showed their hostility by sending a hail of arrows and darts in his direction and attempted to seize a small boat. After the attack had been repulsed the Spanish returned to their ships. After sailing southward they landed and secured a supply of water and firewood, but at this place they had to repel an attack by sixty Indians. A voyage around the Florida Keys took Ponce's men to the western side of Florida where they met a similar reception at the hands of Indians living along the Florida Gulf coast.[11]

In 1562 Jean Ribault and a band of 150 French Huguenot colonists seeking a place to settle where they could practice their faith and not be persecuted or killed, sailed from Havre de Grace to the New World. In May 1562 Ribault moved to a site near the mouth of the Saint John's River where he and his men received a friendly reception from the Indians. The natives indicated a good landing spot, and after the French came ashore the Indians gave them painted deerskins, various types of fish, a feather fan, and a woven palm leaf basket; in exchange, the leader and his advisers received a blue robe trimmed with golden fleur-de-lis and the other Indians were given metal bracelets, mirrors, and knives.[12]

After a short stay the French crossed the Saint John's River to erect a stone marker and received another reception from the assembled Indians. Gifts similiar to those given on the previous day were exchanged and, in addition, pearls and what may have been gold were given to the French by the Indians.[13] After a two days' stay, Ribault and his men sailed northward to Parris Island, South Carolina, where a fort was established, but it was destined to a brief existence which ended when the survivors sailed to England in a crude vessel they built.

Driven by the constant fear that they would be massacred in their own country, the Huguenots regrouped their forces and came back under the leadership of René de Laudonnière in June 1564.[14] Remembering Ribault and his gifts, Athore and his band of Timucuans gave a friendly reception to the three hundred men and four women and presented them with offerings of cornmeal, ears of corn, smoked lizards, and other delicacies, as well as medicinal roots and a limited number of gold and silver ornaments, and showed the French the marker which Ribault had erected.[15] Several Indian leaders and their men from nearby villages visited the site and told Laudonnière about Saturiba, the principal chief of the coastal area around the mouth of the Saint John's River.[16]

Since Saturiba had his scouts watching the French from the moment of their landing, Laudonnière was able to make arrangements for a meeting which culminated in the Indian leader's visit to the partially constructed outpost known as Fort Caroline, where a pact of friendship was arranged. At first Saturiba showed some hostility by inquiring why his province had been selected for the colony and the purpose of the settlement and by closely examining the arms and details of the fort. Observing the blast issued by the brass cannon and the deadly power of the harquebus, a firearm used by some of the French, Saturiba was impressed and he began to realize what a powerful ally fortune had delivered to his province.[17] When Laudonnière asked for assistance in the construction of the triangular-shaped fortification Saturiba sent eighty of his strongest men who spent two days gathering and weaving palm leaves to cover the roof of the armory.[18] Since a very limited amount of food had been brought from France, the Indians helped the French adjust to life in the New World by providing from their own supplies. Laudonnière said that whenever the Indians visited him bringing fish, deer, turkeys, bear cubs, and other products of the country, he gave in exchange hatchets, knives, glass beads, combs, and mirrors. Some time later the Indians discovered that the tips of knives made excellent arrow heads and were eager to exchange food for the worn-out knives of the French.[19]

Although Saturiba did not understand how clumsy the eleven-pound harquebus was, he realized its value as a weapon of terror when first used against a primitive people and sought the use of some French harquebusiers in a campaign to be waged against Utina, a neighboring leader, and the confederation which bore his name.[20] The Indian leader insisted that the pact of friendship which had been agreed upon during Saturiba's visit to Fort Caroline included French involvement as an active ally in the raid against Utina.

Laudonnière turned down the request for immediate aid because his men were needed for the protection of the fort and the construction of two vessels, but he promised help at a future date. Saturiba was not pleased with the French response, for he and his men were ready to move against the enemy and the campaign was commenced without French aid.[21] Saturiba and his followers gained a victory and were able to capture twenty-four of Utina's men. The prisoners were divided equally among the other leaders, but Saturiba in consequence of his position was given thirteen prisoners.

By November 1564 a new development had emerged to complicate matters. Exploring parties were sent into the Florida wilderness and extended contacts were made with Utina and his confederation. Since Laudonnière wanted to win the friendship of Utina, who seemed to control the passageway to the Appalachian Mountains, reputedly rich in gold and silver, he put pressure upon Saturiba to deliver two of his prisoners to the French so that they could return them to Utina.[22] The Timucuan refused to part with his prisoners for he believed Laudonnière could not be trusted, but Laudonnière "wanting to make [this savage] know how dearly this bold bravado of his should cost him" surrounded the Indian leader's hut with twenty soldiers and refused to allow anybody to enter.[23] Alarmed by this show of force, Saturiba surrendered all of the prisoners to the French. After the released captives were able to make their way back to their villages with a French escort, a pact of friendship was negotiated between the Huguenots and Utina. One consequence of this pact was the use of twenty-five French harquebusiers by Utina to gain victory over a neighboring leader named Potanou.

French disillusionment with Utina came about when La

Roche Ferrière discovered while out on a scouting party that actually three leaders—Potanou, Onatheagua, and Oustaca—and not Utina controlled the passageway to the Appalachians.[24] Contact was made with these leaders and gold and silver plates and nuggets of silver were exchanged for cloth, axes, and saws. One leader promised to supply the French with all the gold they needed if they would send one hundred harquebusiers to assist him in a raid, but Laudonnière did not accept the offer.

Although Saturiba was not given assistance for his foray against Utina and, moreover, had been forced to surrender the prisoners he had captured, he and the members of his confederation showed little resentment towards the whites. Perhaps the good relations were due to the excellent beginning inaugurated by Ribault and consequently there developed religious activities, trade, and social contacts between the two groups. Several settlers commenced instruction in the Christian faith to a class which grew to more than two hundred adults and children.[25] The instruction of these Indians was the first case of the Protestant faith being taught to the natives of the United States.

Two items obtained from the forests and savannahs by the Indians were most popular. The whites had observed the preparation and use of sassafras tea and had noted that few persons who drank the tea became ill. According to the Indian recipe the root was sliced and soaked in water until "the water was well colored."[26] The French did not understand that the boiling of the water in preparing the tea killed many germs, but they realized that it was a safe drink. The use of tobacco which was dried and smoked by the Indians was transmitted to the French. One witness gave this account:

> The Floridians when they travel, have a kind of herbe dried who with a cane and a earthern cup in the end with fire and the fried herbes put together doe sucke through the tube the smoke thereof which smoke satisfieth their hunger and therewith they live foure or five days without meat or drink and this all the Frenchmen used for this purpose.[27]

This use of tobacco in 1565 by the French was among the first recorded instances of the smoking of tobacco by the Europeans in the United States.

Since only four women had been included within the ranks of the settlers, the Europeans began to form friendships with the available Indian women. To Laudonnière, who was devoutly religious, those settlers who lived with the Indian girls and did not marry them were either Moors (non-French) or paroled criminals. One enterprising soldier, Pierre Gambré, left Fort Caroline with a supply of inexpensive goods and a trading license to establish a trade with the Indians. Within a year's time he had acquired considerable wealth, a daughter of a leader for a wife, and much influence. But all of this collapsed when Gambré, returning to Fort Caroline for a short visit, was killed by his Indian porter who was motivated partly by revenge and partly by a desire to acquire the goods Gambré was carrying with him.[28]

During the spring and summer of 1565 the French underwent a period of starvation which almost brought about the liquidation of the colony and destroyed much of the friendship they had developed with the neighboring Indians. During the winter of 1564 and 1565 the Timucuans left their semipermanent villages and retired to the woods, leaving the French with no assistance in food procurement. When the colony had first been planned, the colonists were assured that food sufficient for one year would be carried aboard the ships and other supplies would be regularly sent to Florida. Actually only one month's supply of food had been brought to Florida, and no supplies of food arrived during the spring and summer of 1565. The French were ill prepared for the disaster which was fast approaching. None of them knew how to borrow the proper seed corn from the Indians and to prepare their fields for crops or to hunt deer and bison in the woods or fish in the rivers and lakes. Still, much of the hardship could have been avoided had a sufficient quantity of trade goods been provided, but there were only a few items available.

Laudonnière and his men rationed the supply of food in the hope that ships would arrive from France during the spring of

1565. Unfortunately, by May the ships had not arrived, and the settlers were reduced to eating roots and grass. The Indians had returned from the woods, but they were of little help for they had exchanged most of their available corn and beans for French products, and the only food available for trade was fish.

Initially the French Huguenots were able to obtain sufficient food by hunting and trade, but gradually the food problem became acute. At first hundreds of passenger pigeons settled near the fort and were shot as a ready source of food.[29] Later, the widow of a deceased Indian leader who had lived twelve miles to the north of Fort Caroline supplied the French with acorns and corn, but this supply was soon exhausted. A frantic search for food brought about ill feelings, for when the whites could not find any corn or beans in a village, they would set fire to it and mistreat any natives found in the area. Within a short time very few Indians could be seen within three or four miles of the fort.[30]

Aware of the serious food situation both the French and Indians took some harsh measures. Since the course of events indicated that the colony would be abandoned, some French suggested that in order to save their lives one or more Indian leaders should be seized and held until a ransom of food would be paid. Laudonnière refused to listen to this advice, saying that if the Indians knew the desperate state of affairs faced by the French they would gladly trade food for French products. However, when the Indians came in their dugouts to trade, they demanded very high prices—one fish for one shirt—and laughed at the discomfort of the starving men. Although Utina wanted help in a raid against a neighboring leader who had rejected his leadership, he only brought twelve baskets of acorns and two of wild fruit, claiming that all of the remaining corn was needed for planting.[31]

At this point Laudonnière was forced to take decisive action by seizing Utina and his son and demanding food in exchange for his release. Fifty soldiers made their way along the Saint John's River for forty or fifty leagues to the village of Utina, where the Indian leader was easily seized and taken to the boats. In the hope that Utina would be released, fish, acorns, and the black drink were brought to the French, but the supply was insufficient for the need. Some Indians explained that they were certain that Utina would be killed and that only a token amount of food had been offered. In fact, plans were being made to make another son of Utina leader in his place. Some neighboring leaders sent word that if the French killed Utina they would give them all of the food they desired. Even Saturiba asked that Utina be released to him and supplemented his request with gifts of seven baskets of corn and acorns. Nevertheless, most of the promises could not be fulfilled, for corn and beans were needed for planting in the fields. Fish could not be caught or trapped in the rivers, and as a result the French continued to eat roots.

Laudonnière had hoped that the Indian leader would be exchanged for some corn and beans, but since it was the custom of the Timucuans to kill most of the men captured in battle, they did not understand ransom and thought it was an attempt to trap them. After the Indians had tried many times to entice the French into ambushes and failed, an exchange of corn for Utina was made. After the transaction took place and the Frenchmen were carrying the corn back to their ships, they walked into an ambush where two men were killed, twenty-two wounded, and most of the corn was lost. The unusual amount of casualties came about as a result of the Indians learning to shoot their arrows at arms and legs and not at bodies which were protected by armor.[32]

When the corn ripened, the French visited places whenever they heard a crop was available and obtained a limited supply of food. One such expedition went by sea as far north as the Satilla River in Georgia, where a good supply of crushed corn was obtained at a council of Indians from coastal Georgia and Florida. Sometimes in desperation the corn was eaten when it was not yet ripe, and the men became ill.

With the abundance of the ripening corn and beans, relations for the good developed with Saturiba and his people. After learning that the French had given up any hope of maintaining a successful colony and were ready to end their colonial experiment, the Timucuans said that some of their tribe wanted to visit France in order to learn the language and to understand the greatness of the country. They begged Laudonnière to return again to help them against their enemies, to leave Fort Caroline standing, and to leave a boat for use against their enemies. Laudonnière granted all that they desired and prepared to leave Florida.[33]

In July and August of 1565 relief came to the distressed colony in the form of an English visitor and the return of Ribault from France with one thousand men and seven ships. In July 1565 John Hawkins, en route home to England from a voyage to Africa and the West Indies, stopped in Florida. He took pity on the starving Europeans and gave them oil, olives, rice, biscuits, beans, and a ship in exchange for several brass cannon. This supply of food helped sustain the inhabitants of Fort Caroline during the time the colonists were building ships for a return to France.[34] On August 28, 1565 Jean Ribault and his fleet brought food, a fresh supply of manpower, and renewed hope for the colony.

Although Florida had little or no importance as a producer of gold, silver, or animal hides, the peninsula had considerable value to the Spanish for the ships carrying gold from the New World to Spain sailed along the Bahama Channel to Cape Canaveral and thence to the Bermudas and Spain. To the Spaniards, occupation of Northeastern Florida by a non-Spanish, non-Catholic group was intolerable—every effort would be made to remove the intruders.

Philip II, ruler of Spain, selected Pedro Menéndez de Avilés, one of Spain's ablest commanders, to remove the French and establish permanent settlements at strategic locations in Florida. Besides the introduction of livestock, settlement of two or three towns, and development of sugar plantations, the *asiento* or contract presented to Menéndez by Philip contained the information that religious personnel would be carried aboard the ships so that they could instruct the Indians in the principles of the Christian faith and the Indians could "be brought to good usuages and customs."[35]

The Spanish fleet anchored off the northeast Florida coast and Menéndez sent a small group of men ashore to acquire some information from the Indians concerning the French. At first the Indians fled into the wooded area but, when one Spaniard offered presents they returned and indicated that they wanted to see the commander of the fleet.[36] Offers to take the Indians to the ships were refused because they feared capture, but when Menéndez landed, they came from the woods and greeted him. The Spanish gave European articles and food to the Indians and, in return, the natives told Menéndez where the French were located.[37]

After ascertaining the whereabouts of the French, Menéndez and his men attempted an initial attack against the enemy at the mouth of the Saint John's River, but finding the French ships too strong, he returned to the future site of Saint Augustine. A landing was made near the Indian village of Seloy, where a large crowd of friendly Indians received the Spaniards. The reception given by Seloy and his Indians was enthusiastic; in fact, the Indian leader invited the Spanish to use his home and any other accommodations that might be useful. Accordingly, the Spaniards moved in and fortified the "great house" by digging a ditch around it and erecting breastworks of sandy soil and wood about the place. Menéndez attempted to avoid the trouble the French had brought upon themselves by ordering the planting of crops, so that food need not be seized from the Indians.

An attack by overland march was planned against Fort Caroline and two Indians who had been at the French outpost volunteered to lead the raid which culminated in a complete Spanish victory. Although the Timucuan Indians played no role in the attack on the fort, they had a most important function in tracking down, killing, and apprehending of the enemy. When two surviving groups from the French vessels which had been wrecked at Matanzas made their way ashore, the Fresh Water Indians brought word to Saint Augustine, and two Spanish expeditions dispatched to the site and slaughtered the French.[38]

Pedro Menéndez de Avilés had been extremely fortunate in landing at Saint Augustine and meeting an Eastern Timucuan group which was not part of the Saturiba confederation. Had his original plan succeeded, Menéndez would have landed some place on the Saint John's River where he would have had little or no help from the Indians belonging to Saturiba's confederation. By landing at Saint Augustine, Menéndez received much help from the Indians who had not much friendship for the French. Of course, the best place to have landed would have been in Utina's territory.

After Fort Caroline was captured by the Spanish, the outpost was renamed San Mateo and occupied by a Spanish garrison. Relations between the Spaniards and the confederation of tribes led by Saturiba were good; in fact, many of the Timucuans intended to leave their village situated on the bank of the Saint John's River near its mouth and relocate near San Mateo. This good will was crushed when a mutiny was planned by part of the garrison who wanted to leave Florida because they believed that serious trouble in Florida between the Spaniards and the Indians would cause Spain to abandon Florida and recall all of the colonists and soldiers to Spain or the West Indies. In order to promote that trouble they began mistreating and killing the Indians and placed thirty-five defenseless prisoners near an Indian ambush. Of course, the Indians killed all of them.[39]

As a result of this incident and other irritating matters, warfare developed between the Indians and the Spaniards. Indian raiding parties began ambushing food and scouting parties and killing sentries at night, and within a short time they killed an estimated one hundred soldiers. One such party using fire arrows was able to destroy the powder magazine at Saint Augustine. When the Spaniards engaged the Indians they found that their armor and harquebuses were ineffective against fast-moving Indians who could fire five arrows to one blast from a harquebus. The Indians discovered that it took one minute or more to load and fire a harquebus and they were able to fire their arrows and crawl through the grass out of range before the Spaniard was ready for another shot. Eight men from one party of harquebusiers were killed and four were wounded. Finally the Spaniards were forced to burn the houses, destroy the fish weirs, set fire to the cornfields, and punch holes in the canoes to help keep the Indians under control. This type of warfare turned the tide of conflict and soon the Timucuans had lost thirty warriors and sixteen of their leaders had been captured.[40]

The full fury of the Indian war had its effect when Dominique de Gourgues and a French army came to Florida in 1568 and avenged the defeat at Fort Caroline. When Gourgues and his one hundred and eighty men approached the Florida shore at Amelia Island, he found a determined band of Timucuans barring his way. Once the Indians found that their French friends had returned, they showed their joy by dancing about, and in return the French gave them many presents.[41] On the following day Saturiba visited Amelia Island and informed the French where the Spanish fortifications were situated. Saturiba was very happy to see the French, for he claimed that the Spaniards had "made war upon them, burned their homes, cut down their corn, ravished their wives, carried away their daughters, and killed their children."[42] The Indians were of great help to Gourgues when he captured one blockhouse and Fort Caroline and destroyed all material that could not be carried back to the ships.

The warfare waged by the Eastern Timucuans against the French and Spanish was in stark contrast to the reception given to the first settlers of Virginia and New England. At Plymouth the natives had been eliminated by an epidemic, and due to the efforts of Squanto and others a major war did not take place in New England for nearly twenty years. Powhatan's strong control over his Indians in Virginia and the skill in diplomacy exerted by Capt. John Smith prevented a major war from taking place between 1607 and 1618. It was only in Florida that open warfare was waged within a year or so after French settlement.

NOTES

1. Robert F. Spencer et al., *The Native Americans: Prehistory and Ethnology of the North American Indians* (New York: Harper and Row, 1965), p. 431.

2. John R. Swanton, *The Indian Tribes of North America*, Smithsonian

Institution Bureau of American Ethnology Bulletin no. 145 (Washington, D.C., 1952), pp. 114, 141–154.

3. Julian Granberry, "Timucua I: Prosodics and Phonemics of the Mocama District," *International Journal of American Linguistics* 22 (1952): 99.

4. Ripley Bullen places the southern limit of Timucuan territory nearly one hundred miles farther south at the middle of Charlotte Harbor. Ripley P. Bullen, "The Southern Limit of Timucua Territory," *Florida Historical Quarterly* 47 (1969): 414–419.

5. There were more than forty villages in the Utina confederation and thirty villages in the Saturiba confederation. René Laudonnière, "History of Florida," in *The Voyages, Traffiques, and Discoveries of Foreign Voyages*, 10, ed. Richard Hakluyt (New York: E. P. Dutton, 1928), p. 57.

6. For a discussion of Eastern Timucuan population figures, see John M. Goggin, *Space and Time Perspective in Northern St. John's Archaeology Florida*, Yale University Publications in Anthropology no. 47 (New Haven, Conn.: Department of Anthropology, Yale University, 1952) p. 29. Although the name *Timucua* was taken from the confederacy of Utina or Thimoga, it was applied to all of the inhabitants of the noted area. The Spanish practice was to name a tribe or confederation in honor of the highest ranking leader at the time of contact.

7. John R. Swanton, "Aboriginal Culture of the Southeast," *Forty-second Annual Report of the Bureau of American Ethnology to the Secretary of the Smithsonian Institution* (Washington, D.C.: Smithsonian Institution, 1928), p. 679.

8. Three books which have made reproductions of De Bry's engravings published in 1590 include *The New World: The First Pictures of America*, ed. Stefan Lorant (New York: Duell, Sloan and Pearce, 1946); *Settlement of Florida*, comp, Charles E. Bennett (Gainesville: University of Florida Press, 1968); *Southeastern Indians, Life Portraits: A Catalogue of Pictures, 1564–1866*, ed. Emma Lila Fundaburk (1958; reprint ed., Metuchen, N.J.: Scarecrow Reprint, 1969).

9. Jacques Le Moyne, "Narrative," in *Settlement of Florida*, comp. Charles E. Bennett, pp. 62–63.

10. John Sparke, "The Second Voyage Made by the R. W. Sir John Hawkins," in *Early English and French Voyages: Chiefly from Hakluyt, 1534–1608*, ed. Henry Burrage (New York: Scribner's, 1906), p. 110.

11. Frederick T. Davis, "History of Ponce de Leon's Voyages to America," *Florida Historical Quarterly* 14 (1935); 1–49.

12. Laudonnière, "History," p. 17.

13. Jean Ribault, *The Whole and True Discovery of Terra Florida*, ed. David L. Dowd, Floridiana Facsimile and Reprint Series (Gainesville: University of Florida Press, 1964) p. 72.

14. Jean Ribault was imprisoned at this time in the Tower of London.

15. Le Moyne, "Narrative," p. 92; the stone marker was erected at what is now the United States Naval Station, Mayport, Fla.

16. The leaders of the coastal area were relatives and friends of Saturiba. Athore, a very tall son of Saturiba, had married his own mother and had several children. After the marriage had taken place, Saturiba, in turn, married a much younger woman. Le Moyne, "Narrative," p. 18.

17. Le Moyne, "Narrative," p. 95.

18. Laudonnière, "History," p. 54.
19. Sparke, "Second Voyage," p. 43.
20. Le Moyne, "Narrative," p. 95.
21. Laudonnière, "History," p. 62.
22. La Roche Ferrière, a French explorer sent out by Laudonnière, had become very friendly with Utina and was able to deliver to Fort Caroline some gold and pearls.
23. Laudonnière, "History," p. 64.
24. Ibid., pp. 86–87.
25. Woodbury Lowery, *The Spanish Settlements within the Present Limits of the United States: Florida, 1562–1574* (New York: G. P. Putnam's Sons, 1911), p. 78.
26. Andrés G. de Barcia Carballido y Zúñiga, *Chronological History of the Conquest of Florida, 1512–1722,* trans. Anthony Kerrigan (Gainesville: University of Florida Press, 1951), pp. 160–161.
27. Sparke, "Second Voyage," p. 47.
28. Le Moyne, "Narrative," pp. 86–87.
29. Laudonnière, "History," p. 84.
30. Le Moyne, "Narrative," p. 98.
31. Laudonnière, "History," p. 92.
32. Sparke, "Second Voyage," p. 112.
33. Laudonnière, "History," p. 107.
34. Although the French were reduced to the eating of fish bones, they had at least one hundred chickens, twenty barrels of wine, and some sheep at this time and Hawkins enjoyed several excellent meals in Florida. Laudonnière, "History," p. 104.
35. For the agreement and contract signed by Pedro Menéndez de Avilés for the conquest and settlement of Florida see Gonzalo Solís de Merás, *Pedro Menéndez de Avilés, Adelantado, Governor and Captain General of Florida,* ed. and trans. Jeannette Thurber Connor (Deland: Florida State Historical Society, 1923), pp. 259–270.
36. Barcia, *Chronological History,* pp. 81–82.
37. Information gained from French deserters captured in Cuba aided Menéndez in determining the location and size of Fort Caroline.
38. Solís de Merás, *Pedro Menéndez,* pp. 109–115.
39. Ibid., p. 159.
40. Ibid., pp. 233–236.
41. Dominique de Gourgues, "The Recapture of Florida," trans. Jeannette Thurber Connor, in Bennett, *Settlement of Florida,* pp. 209, 212.
42. Ibid., p. 210.

SOURCES CITED

Barcia Carballido y Zúñiga, Andrés G. de, *Chronological History of the Conquest of Florida, 1512–1722.* Translated by Anthony Kerrigan. Gainesville: University of Florida Press, 1951.
Bennett, Charles E., comp. *Settlement of Florida.* Gainesville: University of Florida Press, 1968.

Bullen, Ripley P. "The Southern Limit of Timucua Territory." *Florida Historical Quarterly* 47 (1969): 414–419.

Davis, Frederick T. "History of Ponce de Leon's Voyages to America." *Florida Historical Quarterly* 14 (1935): 1–49.

Fundaburk, Emma Lila. *Southeastern Indians, Life Portraits: A Catalogue of Pictures, 1564–1866.* 1958. Reprint. Metuchen, N.J.: Scarecrow Reprint, 1969.

Goggin, John M. *Space and Time Perspective in Northern St. John's Archaeology Florida.* Yale University Publications in Anthropology no. 47. New Haven, Conn.: Department of Anthropology, Yale University, 1952.

Gourgues, Dominique de. "The Recapture of Florida." Translated by Jeannette Thurber Connor. In *Settlement of Florida,* edited by Charles E. Bennett, pp. 185–228. Gainesville: University of Florida Press, 1968.

Granberry, Julian. "Timucua I: Prosodics and Phonemics of the Mocama District." *International Journal of American Linguistics* 22 (1952): 97–105.

Laudonnière, René. "History of Florida." Translated by Richard Hakluyt. In *The Voyages, Traffiques and Discoveries of Foreign Voyagers,* 10, edited by Richard Hakluyt, pp. 13–134. New York: E. P. Dutton, 1928.

Le Moyne, Jacques. "Narrative." In *Settlement of Florida,* compiled by Charles E. Bennett, pp. 185–227. Gainesville: University of Florida Press, 1968.

Lorant, Stefan, ed. *The New World: The First Pictures of America.* New York: Duell, Sloan and Pearce, 1946.

Lowery, Woodbury, *The Spanish Settlements within the Present Limits of the United States: Florida, 1562–1574.* New York: G. P. Putnam's Sons, 1911.

Ribault, Jean. *The Whole and True Discoverye of Terra Florida.* Edited by David L. Dowd. Floridiana Facsimile and Reprint Series. Gainesville: University of Florida Press, 1964.

Solís De Merás, Gonzalo. *Pedro Menéndez de Avilés, Adelantado, Governor and Captain General of Florida.* Edited and translated by Jeannette Thurber Connor. Deland: Florida State Historical Society, 1923.

Sparke, John. "The Second Voyage Made by the R. W. Sir John Hawkins." In *Early English and French Voyages: Chiefly from Hakluyt, 1534–1608,* Edited by Henry Burrage, pp. 111–132. New York: Scribner's, 1906.

Spencer, Robert F., Jennings, Jesse D., et al. *The Native Americans: Prehistory and Ethnology of the North American Indians.* New York: Harper and Row, 1965.

Swanton, John R. "Aboriginal Culture of the Southeast." *Forty-second Annual Report of the Bureau of American Ethnology to the Secretary of the Smithsonian Institution.* Washington D.C., 1928.

———. *The Indian Tribes of North America.* Smithsonian Institution. Bureau of American Ethnology Bulletin no. 145. Washington, D.C., 1946.

Did a Tuscarora Confederacy Exist?

Douglas W. Boyce

Many people associate the Tuscarora Indians with the Iroquoian Six Nations Confederacy. Others recall their role in the misnamed Tuscarora War of 1711 to 1713, which resulted in large numbers of them fleeing north from their eastern North Carolina homes. Very few anthropologists have done research on the Tuscarora, and only three have anything to say about their early political organization. J. N. B. Hewitt, himself a Tuscarora, worked over fifty years for the Bureau of American Ethnology, leaving a wealth of information in notes. He published however only one major article on the Tuscarora which appeared in the *Handbook of American Indians North of Mexico*. Drawing on historical sources and oral tradition, he says that they were "formerly an important confederation of tribes, [and that] . . . the Tuscarora league was composed of at least three tribal constituent members, each bearing an independent and exclusive appellation."[1]

Anthony F. C. Wallace's research on the Tuscarora began in 1948 and culminated in *The Modal Personality Structure of the Tuscarora Indians* in 1952. He describes them in an historical introduction as being "a loose military league. . . . [they] evidently had leanings toward confederacy, their 'nation' being welded out of several tribal groups." During their war with the colonists from 1711 to 1713 the "Tuscarora themselves were split into pro- and anti-English factions, and a general confusion over the whole situation, shattered the already uncertain unity of Tuscarora society."[2]

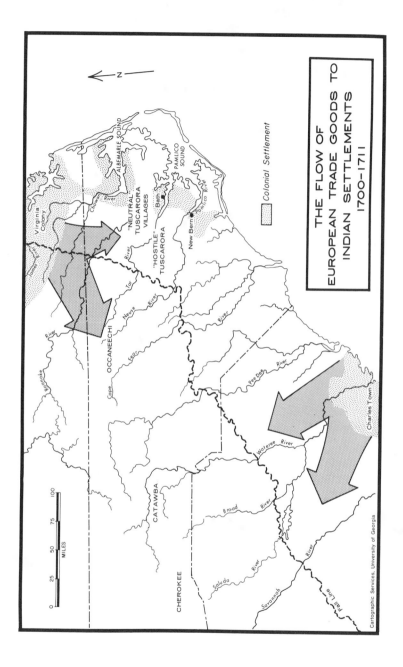

THE FLOW OF
EUROPEAN TRADE GOODS TO
INDIAN SETTLEMENTS
1700–1711

Colonial Settlement

N

MILES
0   25   50   75   100

Virginia Colony

James River

Chowan River

ALBEMARLE SOUND

"NEUTRAL TUSCARORA VILLAGES"

"HOSTILE" TUSCARORA

Bath

PAMLICO SOUND

New Bern

Pamlico River

Roanoke River

Tar River

Neuse River

Cape Fear River

OCCANEECHI

Pee Dee River

Wateree River

Charles Town

CATAWBA

Broad River

Saluda River

Savannah River

CHEROKEE

Fall Line

Cartographic Services, University of Georgia

David Landy in a 1958 article states that they "operated as a relatively successful confederation of several Carolina tribes. . . . During this period of ascendancy, the Chiefs' Council, whatever its actual structure then, must have functioned with a high degree of integration and political effectiveness. Between 1711 and 1713, the fierce Tuscarora War decimated the tribes and emasculated their economic and political power in relation to whites as well as other Indian tribes."[3]

Two points made by these scholars need to be scrutinized in detail: (1) that the Tuscarora were organized as a confederation of tribes before 1711, and (2) that this confederation was split by factionalism during the war that broke out in that year. It is difficult to formulate satisfactory definitions of political behavior and organization. For the present however a tribe may be considered to be a group of one or more communities possessing a name, a territory, and a group decision-making mechanism; usually it acts independently as a unit in matters of intergroup relations. When two or more tribes join together as equal and autonomous groups, sharing a common political organization that maintains their internal distinctness, we may refer to them as a tribal confederacy. "Factionalism," another important concept, may be defined as overt, unregulated conflict which develops between two or more segments within a group where these segments are not persistent, autonomous units and do not have distinct identities nor organizations with specific procedures and regulations.[4] In other words conflict between clans, villages, tribes, or other conventional political divisions within a confederacy is institutionally based political behavior, but it is not factionalism. Before examining the evidence directly related to these aspects of Tuscarora political organization it will be helpful to survey the general development of colonial settlement and Indian trade in the Carolina-Virginia area.

The early years of the seventeenth century in Virginia and the Carolinas saw the founding of the first successful English settlement at Jamestown. The preceding one hundred years witnessed the explorers, Verrazzano, DeSoto, and others, who touched the seaward and western fringes of the Carolinas. The later attempts of the English to establish themselves on Roanoke Island and finally their faltering success in the Chesapeake Bay were all witnessed by the local indigenous populations; and certainly word of some or all of these ventures rapidly spread to the more distant interior people of the area.

The Virginia Indian trade became established initially with the villages near the English plantations and was extended to the upper Chesapeake Bay area from the 1620s to the 1630s. As these areas became settled by colonists, traders turned westward along the major rivers and eventually, at midcentury, they went south. The lack of a waterway back to an established market made agricultural developments in the North Carolina piedmont impossible, but the increased availability of horses for use as pack animals opened the way for the traders. Initial expansion in a southerly direction went not toward the Tuscarora but toward the Occaneechi, and before Bacon's Rebellion in 1676, contacts had already been made with distant Cherokee villages.[5]

At about this same time Indian trade operations from Charles Town began to expand at an impressive rate. The lack of mountain barriers to their west, and the minimal resistance from Indian groups that were potential middlemen seems to have given them the edge over their Virginia counterparts.

North Carolina played almost no part in the development of this trade. Initial white settlement came in the late 1650s and early 1660s in the Albemarle area. It was in every respect a frontier colony. Trade with the Indians was on a local level, since as Verner Crane points out, to do more required "capital accumulations of prosperous planters and merchants, and direct mercantile connections with England."[6] North Carolina lacked both of these. The colony's growth was slow, and expansion outside of the Albemarle area did not begin until after 1691, when a group of Huguenots settled on the Pamlico, followed in 1704 by the town of Bath, and a French colony on the Trent in 1708. The Palatine settlement of New Bern was

established at the confluence of the Neuse and Trent rivers in
1710, and the next few years found the North Carolina colonists embroiled in a war with many of the native inhabitants
including a number of Tuscarora villages.

The Tuscarora were peripherally located with respect to
English colonial expansion, and this is reflected by the fact
that they were not mentioned in the historical record until
1650.[7] Even for forty years after 1650 there are only several
notes based on brief visits at some of the fringe villages or an
occasional complaint concerning them in Virginia Council and
House of Burgesses records. References by Edward Bland,
Francis Yeardley, John Lederer, and George Fox before 1675
describe the Tuscarora as a powerful nation ruled by a supreme emperor.[8] But their encounters with the people were
brief, or in the case of Yeardley a secondhand report, and such
descriptions probably tell us more about the observers than
about those observed. As Walter Miller has pointed out for
the Fox Indians, the European colonist tended to apply his
own concept of authority to the indigenous people he encountered.[9] Thus a village chief or headman acting as host for his
people was automatically endowed with the powers of a European monarch who might receive guests of state in a similar
manner.

After 1675, as source materials become progressively more
detailed, it is possible to reconstruct a more accurate picture
of Tuscarora political organization. From private letters and
the colonial records describing Indian-white disputes, it becomes clear that the Tuscarora village was the primary political unit. For example William Byrd wrote to Lord Effingham
10 June 1689 after a Tuscarora had been killed, saying that he
expected to meet with "ye great men of the Town & the relations of ye slain man."[10]

On 14 October 1707 Jeremiah Pate of New Kent County,
Virginia, was supposedly killed by five to ten Tuscaroras. Messengers sent to one Tuscarora village returned saying they had
been assured that the guilty men from that town would be sent
to Williamsburg. As the court waited for the others who were
accused to be brought in, all trade with the Tuscaroras was

stopped. Six months after Pate's death, several traders reported that many of the Tuscarora villages would gladly deliver the other suspects, but they had no authority in the matter because the villages to which the fugitives belonged refused to give them up. During the next year trade south of the James River in Virginia and North Carolina was halted because goods were still flowing to the Tuscaroras through the Nottoway, Meherrin, and frontier settlers. The Tuscaroras never complied with Virginia's demands, but in late April 1709 pressure on the Virginia Council from irate merchants was so great that all trade was reopened.[11]

During the war of 1711 to 1713 negotiations were often conducted between colonial officials and representatives of eight neutral villages. On 15 October 1711 Governor Spotswood of Virginia met with five Tuscarora "great men" who claimed to represent these eight villages, saying they were authorized only to hear the governor's proposals and then would have to consult each town. Although agreements were made the following December by three individuals claiming to have full authority, later it was revealed that this unanimity was not as complete as it appeared to be; and in the months that followed, representatives from several of the villages expressed their disapproval.[12]

Col. James Moore led a force of Indians and whites from South Carolina during the winter of 1712 and 1713 to subdue the "hostile" Indians, prompting at least five of the neutral villages to flee to Virginia. On reports that these Tuscaroras had attacked frontier settlements, Spotswood sent out fifty tributary Indians of Virginia led by two traders who

> found them dispers'd in small parties upon the head of Roanoke [River], and about the Mountains in very miserable condition, without any habitation or provision of Corne for their Subsistence, but living like wild beasts on what ye Woods afforded, in dispair whether to return to their old Settlements in No. Carolina and run the risque of being knock'd in the head by the English and So. Carolina Indians or to submit themselves to ye Senecas, who had made them large offers of Assistance to revenge them-

selves on the English, upon condition of incorporating with them.[13]

Even in this extremely disruptive situation village identities were maintained. Governor Spotswood's meeting with the representatives of one such group illustrates, in a unique firsthand manner, the primacy of the village and the generalized, representative basis for authority.

> We are sent by our Town called Tervanihow. . . . Do you come from y'r own Town. From none but their own Town. . . . [They came] to hear what the Gov'r says or has to propose & upon their return, their Great men will come in to conclude. . . . Do they desire to live in ye same manner as our Tributarys do, and what do they mean by this proposal. They cannot answer it without consulting their Town—they may tell lyes and their people may be offended with them and not stand to their offers. Why do they rather desire to live here than to return to their old Settlem'ts in North Carolina. They can't say till they know it from their people.[14]

There are other less explicit summaries of such exchanges, but nearly all have several things in common. First, in meetings with colonial officials the Tuscaroras sent two to five men as representatives no matter how many villages were involved. Second, authority to confirm treaties or concur on solutions to differences was based on the agreement of each village. Beyond that the people of each village and not the chief or council are mentioned as being the basis for this authority.[15]

The writings of Lawson and Graffenried provide more detail than the colonial records concerning the actual functioning of the Tuscarora political organization. From their accounts the council clearly emerges as the most important governing or decision-making unit. The morning after Graffenried and Lawson were taken prisoners and brought to the Tuscarora village of Catechna, a council was held, the members of which came from several different households. That evening a broader level council met. Included were the chiefs or headmen of neighboring Tuscarora and non-Tuscarora villages. They met in an open area, seated in a ring around a fire where issues were debated at length before reaching a decision.[16] In the days to follow, Lawson was killed and Graffenried signed a treaty committing him and the New Bern colony to neutrality in order to save his own life. Several weeks later, after Governor Spotswood threatened the intervention of Virginia, Graffenried was taken by four guards to the Tuscarora town of Tasqui, where representatives from the neutral Tuscarora villages were meeting in a circle around the central village fire.

> The council which consisted of the chiefs of the Tuscarora Nation was sitting around on the ground. . . . After a hearing, I was found and declared innocent, and it was decided to comply with the desires of the Governor of Virginia [to free me]. . . . The four Indians of Catechna would not agree to that . . . pretending that they dare not do it without the consent of the other kings and chiefs, yet promising to let me loose as soon as the king and council should be together.[17]

Graffenried's descriptions of council sessions are the only ones we have for this period of Tuscarora cultural history. Beyond this other features of internal sociopolitical organization cannot be adequately documented. There are only a few brief historical references to matrilineal descent, and the Tuscarora chiefs may or may not have been hereditary.[18] Furthermore there is no evidence that these chieftainships were held by individuals representing specific clans, with successors chosen by clan matrons, as was the case later in New York. Women referred to as *queens* served in some political and ceremonial capacities; but their significance cannot be determined since they are mentioned only in passing.[19] Further food for speculation is provided by a reference to a "young" Tuscarora village chief and the apparently close relationship of another village chief to his sister's son.[20] These are all unfortunately too insubstantial for even a rudimentary understanding of most sociopolitical spheres.

At any rate Graffenried said the council at Tasqui was made

up of "the chiefs of the Tuscarora Nation." Clearly the chiefs of the "hostile" Tuscarora towns were not present. Was this due to conflict between villages or factional splits which developed during the war? Was there really a high degree of integration and political effectiveness on a confederacy or even tribal level? During the initial month after Graffenried and Lawson were captured and hostilities broke out, apparently no councils were held involving all the Tuscarora villages, since the council at Tasqui was the first opportunity the neutral villages had to express their opinion in the matter. Graffenried's statement that the Tasqui council represented the Tuscarora Nation merely points out how ambiguously the Europeans applied the term *nation* to the Indians in the seventeenth and eighteenth centuries. Most often it was a convenient category applied to groups that appeared ethnically distinctive to European observers.

In terms of the historical record of the period I suggest there were, instead of a Tuscarora confederacy, at least two major alliances, each containing villages called Tuscarora by the colonists. On the one hand the "hostile" alliance included several Tuscarora villages, as well as those of the Coree, Neusiok, Woccon, Pamlico, Bear River, and Machapunga. The neutral villages were primarily Tuscaroran, but their alliance also included the Shakoris, Chickahominies, and probably the Meherrins and Nottoways.[21] The immediate causes for the development of these alliances is to be found in the political organization of the Indians and the nature of the colonists' interaction with them.

White settlements began to expand along the Trent, Neuse, and Pamlico rivers in North Carolina after 1690. Little care was taken with the indigenous populations living there. As a result in 1703 war broke out between the settlers and the Corees. In February 1704 a group of whites living near the Neuse River pleaded with the North Carolina Council to send them help. They fearfully noticed the increased interaction of nearby disgruntled Tuscarora and Bear River villages.[22]

As coastal Indian villages were displaced, many moved into

territory occupied by the more southern Tuscaroras. Unlike
Virginia, in North Carolina there were no regulations pro-
hibiting relationships between whites and Indians, and nearly
every settler kept a few trade goods on hand.[23] He had to buy
them from Virginia, for the most part, and since he wanted to
make a profit his prices were much higher than those of the
licensed professional Virginia trader. The dissatisfaction of
those Indians living near the lower Neuse River is in marked
contrast to the more northerly Tuscarora villages, who in fact
aided the colonists against them. One point of the treaty concluded between Virginia and the neutral villages suggests the
reason. "Upon their performance of their engagements to this
Government, a peace shall be concluded with them, and a free
trade again opened between this Colony and their towns, and
likewise that according to their desire this Government will
interpose that no unjust Encroachments be made upon their
Lands by the Inhabitants of North Carolina."[24] Obviously
satisfied with things as they had been before the disruption
of war the neutral villages hoped all would be returned to
normal as soon as possible. Graffenried wrote "there were seven
villages [other references say eight] of the Tuscarora . . .
[which] were somewhat farther distant, more beyond [toward]
Virginia, and are loyal yet, keeping their loyalty on the account
of trade. These . . . villages hold the others in this region in
certain bounds and submission."[25] By the late seventeenth
century Virginia traders were still trying to compete with South
Carolina for the southwestern trade with the Cherokees and
Catawbas, and these seven or eight Tuscarora villages must
have been able to capture the middleman position in the flow
of goods south of the James River to nearby North Carolina
Indians. To go a step farther an undated memorial (probably
1718) sent by the Virginia Indian Company to Governor
Spotswood attests that between 1709 and 1711 there had "been
no Trade carried on from hence with any forreign Indians, the
Tuscaruros only excepted."[26] This idea is not new. Several
statements of Lawson's are often cited to show that the Tuscaroras monopolized trade before 1711.[27] It has always been

assumed that the entire Tuscarora Nation, league, confederacy, or whatever held this position. But we now see that it was clearly a limited number of villages.

This commerce was conducted using not the well-known Occaneechi "trading path," but a path parallel to or east of the fall line (see map), perhaps the same route Lewis Binford has suggested for Bland's trip to the Tuscaroras in 1650.[28] In December 1711 the Saponi and Occaneechi, apparently hoping to gain some control of this trade while the Tuscarora were concerned with the war, asked the Virginia government for a piece of land "on the Northside of Meherine River above the Tuscaruro trading path." A year and a half later, in 1713, one of the refugee Tuscarora villages which fled to Virginia expressed a desire to be placed "on Roanoke River near the trading path called Weecacana."[29]

The primacy of the village in the area of territorial control and utilization can be directly related to the deerskin trade, and it also suggests the importance of the village unit in other realms. Each village included a number of agricultural hamlets of several small multinuclear family structures with surrounding farmlands and a cluster of similarly undifferentiated cabins near an open ceremonial and council area. The limited demographic data suggest that in 1710 there were fifteen Tuscarora villages with an average population of three hundred to five hundred per village.[30] This made each village structurally and in many ways politically equivalent to the one-village "nations" living around them.

Tuscarora food production followed an annual cycle. In late fall entire villages with the exception of a few old people moved to hunting quarters. Lawson found one of these within a day's walk of their permanent village in 1701. That this pattern was not new is shown by the fact that in the winter of 1653 and 1654, Yeardley's men found a Tuscarora village in a hunting quarter. The village chief offered to take them to his permanent town, but because their interpreter was sick, they declined. The Tuscaroras Lawson encountered were finding game to be scarce.[31] To counteract this and perhaps better compete in the market economy of the fur trade, hunting quarters were established by some Tuscaroras in Virginia. As early as 1681 Tuscaroras were trading at a fort on the Rappahannock River near present-day Fredericksburg.[32] Complaints came from Henrico County in 1693, and more complaints came in 1699 and 1702 from colonists and tributary Indians along the upper Appomattox River who relied on the game in those areas for their own subsistence.[33] Obviously the agricultural lands, central village areas, and hunting territories were of primary importance to each village. An indication of the extent to which peripheral lands were felt to be "owned" is expressed in the depositions of the North Carolina–Virginia boundary case. The testimony of Nansemond, Nottoway, and Meherrin Indians describes the sale of a plot of land bounded by the Roanoke and Chowan rivers to the Weanock Indians. Two village chiefs or headmen, probably representing their people, made the final arrangements. This is reminiscent of the treaty between the neutral Tuscaroras and the colony of North Carolina signed in November 1712 and another with Virginia in the following year.[34] The name of every participating village is listed along with their representatives.

If there were no Tuscarora confederacy, then what is the basis for its presumed existence? One reason stems from the misuse of historical literature. With little regard for the writers' European concepts of authority, phrases such as *Tuscarora Nation* have been assumed to indicate not just a multivillage organization but a confederation of tribes as well. Hewitt perhaps made this error but draws also on oral tradition for evidence of a tribal league. Later he readily admits that there "are no data, other than those furnished by tradition and analogy . . . as to the organization of the Tuscarora Confederation."[35] Oral tradition can be a useful tool in unraveling the past, as Jan Vansina has demonstrated,[36] but great care must be exercised. Naturally the Tuscarora characterized the past in terms of their present situation, as a member of a confederacy. For example, the traditional history of the Six Nations, written in 1825 by Tuscarora David Cusick, describes the Iroquois as a confederation of tribes with origins just subsequent to their mythical creation. According to Cusick's chronology this was the political structure of the Iroquois, with the exception of brief splits, for fifteen hundred years before Columbus and for their entire history as tribal entities.[37]

A. L. Kroeber has suggested that

> more often than not in native North America the landowning and sovereign political society was not what we usually call "the tribe," but smaller units [bands or villages]. . . . What are generally denominated tribes really are small nationalities, possessing essentially uniform speech and customs and therefore an accompanying sense of likeness and likemindedness. . . . Each owned a particular territory rather than that the nationality owned the over-all territory. Ordinarily, the nationality . . . was only an aggregate of miniature sovereign states normally friendly to one another.[38]

There is little or no historical evidence for a Tuscarora confederacy. On the contrary, the record suggests that the village was the most effectively organized political unit. Each apparently had a representative council and chief. Not only was territory in the control of each village; but basic decisions and goals were determined at this level also. Membership of a village in an alliance seemed to be maintained only as long as the goals of the village were held in common by the others. The Tuscarora alliances which existed before 1713 appear to have been more the result of mutual village cooperation in the face of colonial expansion and trade activities, rather than factional splits within an integrated confederacy.

NOTES

1. J[ohn] N. B. Hewitt, "Tuscarora," in *Handbook of American Indians North of Mexico,* ed. Frederick Webb Hodge, Smithsonian Institution, Bureau of American Ethnology Bulletin no. 30, 2 vols. (Washington, D.C., 1907–1910) , 2: 842.

2. Anthony F. C. Wallace, *The Modal Personality Structure of the Tuscarora Indians,* Smithsonian Institution, Bureau of American Ethnology Bulletin no. 150 (Washington, D.C., 1952) , pp. 14–15.

3. David Landy, "Tuscarora Tribalism and National Identity," *Ethnohistory* 5 (1958) : 263–264.

4. Anthony F. C. Wallace, "Political Organization and Land Tenure among the Northeastern Indians, 1600–1830," *Southwestern Journal of Anthropology* 13 (1957) : 304; Ralph W. Nicholas, "Factions: A Comparative Approach," in *Political Systems and the Distribution of Power,* ed. Michael Banton, Association of Social Anthropologists of the Commonwealth Monograph no. 2 (London: Tavistock, 1965), pp. 27–29.

5. Wesley Frank Craven, *The Southern Colonies in the Seventeenth Century, 1607–1689, A History of the South,* eds. Wendell Holmes Stephenson and E. Merton Coulter, 10 vols. (Baton Rouge: Louisiana State University Press, 1949), 1: 196–198, 369–370; Abraham Wood, "Letter of Abraham Wood to John Richards August 22, 1674," in *The First Explorations of the Trans-Allegheny Region by the Virginians, 1650–1674,* eds. Clarence Walworth Alvord and Lee Bidgood (Cleveland: Clark, 1912), pp. 210–227.

6. Verner W. Crane, *The Southern Frontier, 1670–1732* (Ann Arbor: University of Michigan Press, 1929), p. 158.

7. Herbert Richard Paschal ("The Tuscarora Indians in North Carolina," M.A. thesis, University of North Carolina, Chapel Hill, 1953, pp. 16–21) and Lewis R. Binford ("An Ethnohistory of the Nottoway, Meherrin, and Weanock Indians of Southeastern Virginia," *Ethnohistory* 14, 1967, 123–125) have suggested the Tuscaroras were the Mangoaks spoken of by Lane, Smith, and others in the early Roanoke and Jamestown documents. While this may be true it is not relevant to the problem posed in this paper, since they were only briefly contacted and there is so little ethnographic information concerning them.

8. Edward Bland, "The Discovery of New Brittaine, 1650," in *Narratives of Early Carolina, 1650–1708,* ed. Alexander S. Salley (New York: Scribner's, 1911), p. 9; Francis Yeardley, "Francis Yeardley's Narrative of Excursions into Carolina, 1654," in *Narratives of Carolina,* ed. Salley, p. 27; John Lederer, "The Discoveries in Three Several Marches from Virginia to the West of Carolina, 1669–1670," in *First Explorations by Virginians,* eds. Alvord and Bidgood, p. 162; George Fox, *Selections from the Epistles of George Fox* (Cambridge, Mass.: New England Yearly Meeting of Friends, 1879), p. 154.

9. Walter Miller, "Two Concepts of Authority," *American Anthropologist* 57 (1955): 271–289.

10. William Stanard, ed., "Letters of William Byrd, First," *The Virginia Magazine of History and Biography* 26 (1918): 28.

11. William P. Palmer et al., eds., *Calendar of Virginia State Papers and Other Manuscripts, 1652–1781,* 11 vols. (Richmond: Superintendent of Public Printing, 1875–1893), 1: 123; H[enry] R[ead] McIlwaine, ed., *Executive Journals of the Council of Colonial Virginia,* 5 vols. (Richmond: Virginia State Library, 1925–1945), 3: 158, 165, 171, 200, 211, 214.

12. R[obert] A[lonzo] Brock, ed., *The Official Letters of Alexander Spotswood,* 2 vols. (Richmond: Virginia Historical Society, 1887), 1: 121; William L. Saunders, Walter Clark, and Stephen B. Weeks, eds., *The Colonial and State Records of North Carolina,* 30 vols. (Raleigh: Printer to the State, 1886–1914), 1: 815; McIlwaine, *Executive Journals,* 3: 320; idem, ed., *Journals of the House of Burgesses of Virginia,* 12 vols. (Richmond: Virginia State Library, 1905–1915), 3: 15.

13. Brock, *Letters of Spotswood,* 2: 42.

14. William Stanard, ed., "Examination of Indians, 1713 (?)," *Virginia Magazine of History and Biography* 19 (1911): 272, 274.

15. Elsewhere I have discussed the general cultural basis for authority (Douglas W. Boyce, "Notes on Tuscarora Political Organization, 1650–1713," M.A. thesis, University of North Carolina, Chapel Hill, 1971, pp. 13–25).

16. Vincent H. Todd, ed., *Christoph von Graffenried's Account of the Founding of New Bern* (Raleigh: North Carolina Historical Commission, 1920), pp. 264–266.

17. Ibid., pp. 272–273.

18. Ibid., p. 245; John Lawson, *Lawson's History of North Carolina*, ed. Frances Latham Harriss (Richmond: Garett and Massie, 1937), p. 207.

19. William Stanard, ed., "The Indians of Southern Virginia, 1650–1711: Depositions in the Virginia and North Carolina Boundary Case," *Virginia Magazine of History and Biography* 7 (1900): 350; ibid. 8 (1901): 10; Todd, *Graffenried's Account*, p. 277.

20. Stanard, "Examination of Indians," p. 273; Saunders, Clark, and Weeks, *Colonial Records*, 2: 50.

21. Todd, *Graffenried's Account*, p. 270; Saunders, Clark, and Weeks, *Colonial Records*, 1: 875; McIlwaine, *Executive Journals*, 3: 295.

22. J[ames] R. B. Hathaway, ed., "War Declared against the Core & Nynee Indians, 1703," *North Carolina Historical and Genealogical Register* 2 (1901): 204; idem, "Relating to the Indians, 1703," ibid. 2 (1901): 194.

23. Saunders, Clark, and Weeks, *Colonial Records*, 1: 828.

24. McIlwaine, *Executive Journals*, 3: 295. North Carolina Indians had more than colonial land-grabbing and unequal trade opportunities about which to complain. Slavery was a very real problem (Hewitt, "Tuscarora," 2: 843–845). The extent to which it, or other aggravations, may be related to the alignments of various Indian groups outlined here cannot presently be determined. The factors I emphasize may not be the primary ones, but they do have some significance and, unlike the other possibilities, can be documented.

25. Todd, *Graffenried's Account*, p. 276.

26. "The Memorial of the Virginia Indian Company to the Hon[ble] Alexander Spotswood His Majestes Lieu[t] Governor & Commander in Chief of the Colony & Dominion of Virginia" [n.d.], Fulham Palace Papers Relating to the American Colonies, 1626–1824, microfilm reel 5, vol. 14, p. 254, Southern Historical Collection, University of North Carolina, Chapel Hill.

27. Lawson, *History of North Carolina*, pp. 57, 221, 238.

28. Binford, "Nottoway Indians," pp. 125–133.

29. McIlwaine, *Executive Journals*, 3: 296; Standard, "Examination of Indians," p. 274.

30. Boyce, "Tuscarora Political Organization," pp. 13–15.

31. Lawson, *History of North Carolina*, pp. 58–60; Yeardley, "Excursions into Carolina," p. 27.

32. Fairfax Harrison, "Western Explorations in Virginia between Lederer and Spotswood," *Virginia Magazine of History and Biography* 30 (1922): 326.

33. McIlwaine, *Journals of the House of Burgesses of Virginia*, 2: 454; Palmer et al., *State Papers*, 1: 65; McIlwaine, *Executive Journals*, 2: 275.

34. Stanard, "Indians of Southern Virginia," 7: 350; ibid. 8: 5–8, 10; "Preliminary Articles . . . agreed upon this 25th day of Novr Ano Dm 1712 Between Tom Blount, Saroonha, Heunthanohneh, Chenntharunthoo—Nawoonttootseree Chief Men of Severale of ye Tuskarora Towns for and on behalf of themselves & the Towns of Eukuskusreunt Rarookahoo, Tostohant Rauroota, Tarhuntha Kenta Tohorooka Juninits & Caunookohos of ye own part And the Honble Thos Pollock Esqr Presid^t & ye rest of ye Council for & on behalf of themselves and this Government of North Carolina," Indians, 1712–1923, North Carolina Department of Archives and History, Raleigh; Palmer et al., *State Papers*, 1: 173.

35. Hewitt, "Tuscarora," 2: 842, 849.

36. Jan Vansina, *Oral Tradition: A Study in Historical Methodology* (Chicago: Aldine, 1965).

37. David Cusick, "David Cusick's Sketches of Ancient History of the Six Nations," in *The Iroquis Trail, or Foot-prints of the Six Nations, in Customs, Traditions, and History,* ed. William M. Beauchamp (Fayettville, N.Y.: Recorder Print, 1892), pp. 11–13.

38. A[lfred] L. Kroeber, "Nature of the Land-Holding Group," *Enthohistory* 2 (1955): 303.

SOURCES CITED

Binford, Lewis R. "An Ethnohistory of the Nottoway, Meherrin, and Weanock Indians of Southeastern Virginia." *Ethnohistory* 14 (1967): 103–218.

Bland, Edward. "The Discovery of New Brittaine, 1650." In *Narratives of Early Carolina, 1650–1708,* edited by Alexander S. Salley, pp. 1–19. New York: Scribner's, 1911.

Boyce, Douglas W. "Notes on Tuscarora Political Organization, 1650–1713." M.A. thesis, University of North Carolina, Chapel Hill, 1971.

Brock, R[obert] A[lonzo], ed. *The Official Letters of Alexander Spotswood.* 2 vols. Richmond: Virginia Historical Society, 1887.

Chapel Hill. Southern Historical Collection. Fulham Palace Papers Relating to the American Colonies, 1626–1824.

Crane, Verner W. *The Southern Frontier, 1670–1732.* Ann Arbor: University of Michigan Press, 1929.

Craven, Wesley Frank. *The Southern Colonies in the Seventeenth Century, 1607–1689.* Vol. 1. *A History of the South,* edited by Wendell Holmes Stephenson and E. Merton Coulter. 10 vols. Baton Rouge: Louisiana State University Press, 1949.

Cusick, David. "David Cusick's Sketches of Ancient History of the Six Nations." In *The Iroquois Trail, or Foot-prints of the Six Nations, in Customs, Traditions, and History,* edited by William M. Beauchamp, pp. 1–37. Fayettville, N.Y.: Recorder Print. 1892.

Fox, George. *Selections from the Epistles of George Fox.* Cambridge, Mass.: New England Yearly Meeting of Friends, 1879.

Harrison, Fairfax. "Western Explorations in Virginia between Lederer and Spotswood." *Virginia Magazine of History and Biography* 30 (1922): 323–334.

Hathaway, J[ames] R. B., ed. "Relating to the Indians, 1703." *North Carolina Historical and Genealogical Register* 2 (1901): 193–194.

———. "War Declared against the Core & Nynee Indians, 1703." *North Carolina Historical and Genealogical Register* 2 (1901): 204.

Hewitt, J[ohn] N. B. "Tuscarora." In *Handbook of American Indians North of Mexico*, edited by Frederick Webb Hodge, 2: 842–853. Smithsonian Institution, Bureau of American Ethnology Bulletin no. 30, 2 vols. Washington, D.C., 1907–1910.

Kroeber, A[lfred] L. "Nature of the Land-Holding Group." *Ethnohistory* 2 (1955): 303–314.

Landy, David. "Tuscarora Tribalism and National Identity." *Ethnohistory* 5 (1958): 250–284.

Lawson, John. *Lawson's History of North Carolina*. Edited by Frances Latham Harriss. Richmond: Garett and Massie, 1937.

Lederer, John. "The Discoveries in Three Several Marches from Virginia to the West of Carolina." In *The First Explorations of the Trans-Allegheny Region by the Virginians, 1650–1674*, edited by Clarence Walworth Alvord and Lee Bidgood, pp. 135–171. Cleveland: Clark, 1912.

McIlwaine, H[enry] R[ead], ed. *Executive Journals of the Council of Colonial Virginia*. 5 vols. Richmond: Virginia State Library, 1925–1945.

———. *Journals of the House of Burgesses of Virginia*. 12 vols. Richmond: Virginia State Library, 1905–1915.

Miller, Walter. "Two Concepts of Authority." *American Anthropologist* 57 (1955): 271–289.

Nicholas, Ralph W. "Factions: A Comparative Approach." In *Political Systems and the Distribution of Power*, edited by Michael Banton, pp. 21–61. Association of Social Anthropologists of the Commonwealth Monograph no. 2. London: Tavistock, 1965.

Palmer, William P.; McRae, Sherwin; Colston, Raleigh; and Flournoy, H. W., eds. *Calendar of Virginia State Papers and Other Manuscripts, 1652–1781*. 11 vols. Richmond: Superintendent of Public Printing, 1875–1893.

Paschal, Herbert Richard, Jr. "The Tuscarora Indians in North Carolina." M.A. thesis, University of North Carolina, Chapel Hill, 1953.

Raleigh. North Carolina Department of Archives and History. Indians, 1712–1923.

Saunders, William L.; Clark, Walter; and Weeks, Stephen B., eds. *The Colonial and State Records of North Carolina*. 30 vols. Raleigh: Printer to the State, 1886–1914.

Stanard, William, ed. "Examination of Indians, 1713 (?)." *Virginia Magazine of History and Biography* 19 (1911): 272-275.

———. "The Indians of Southern Virginia, 1650–1711: Depositions of the Virginia and North Carolina Boundary Case." *Virginia Magazine of History and Biography* 7 (1900): 337–358; ibid. 8 (1901): 1–11.

———. "Letters of William Byrd, First." *Virginia Magazine of History and Biography* 26 (1918): 17–31, 124–134, 247–259, 388–392.

Todd, Vincent H., ed. *Christoph von Graffenried's Account of the Founding of New Bern*. Raleigh: North Carolina Historical Commission, 1920.

Vansina, Jan. *Oral Tradition: A Study in Historical Methodology*. Chicago: Aldine, 1965.

Wallace, Anthony F. C. *The Modal Personality Structure of the Tuscarora*

Indians. Smithsonian Institution. Bureau of American Ethnology Bulletin no. 150. Washington, D.C., 1952.

———. "Political Organization and Land Tenure among the Northeastern Indians, 1600–1830." *Southwestern Journal of Anthropology* 13 (1957) : 310–321.

Wood, Abraham. "Letter of Abraham Wood to John Richards August 22, 1674." In *The First Explorations of the Trans-Allegheny Region by the Virginians, 1650–1674*, edited by Clarence Walworth Alvord and Lee Bidgood, pp. 210–227. Cleveland: Clark, 1912.

Yeardley, Francis. "Francis Yeardley's Narrative of Excursions into Carolina, 1654." In *Narratives of Early Carolina, 1650–1708*, edited by Alexander S. Salley pp. 25–29. New York: Scribner's, 1911.

The Southern Indians
in the War for
American Independence
1775-1783

James H. O'Donnell III

At the outbreak of the War for American Independence, the Indian tribes living along the western frontiers of the colonies had reason to be concerned. In the ten years before the Revolution, schemes by frontiersmen and speculators for grabbing Indian lands had been rampant. War now might mean more demands for land, particularly if the colonials emerged victorious, for their land hunger seemingly could not be satisfied. While the tribal leaders in the past preferred to play off one proponent of war against another for the good of the tribe, care now had to be taken, for there was the simple and basic matter that their lands and lives were at stake. Since choosing sides was indeed a calculated risk, most tribes waited and watched for more than a year after the war began.

It was in the South that the warriors struck first. By the spring of 1776 the Cherokees were faced with the unhappy predicament of the continued encroachment by settlers on lands too close to their villages. Cherokee leaders had hoped that the sale to the Transylvania speculators in 1775 would give them breathing room for a time, but the settlers could not be satisfied. In the western stretches of the Carolinas and Georgia the frontiersmen pushed up the rivers into the Cherokee lands, ignoring threats from the tribe and warnings from royal officials. West of the mountains the Overhill Cherokees enjoyed no sanctuary because of their transmontane location. Moving south along the valleys and west through gaps, settlers had entered Eastern Tennessee, again in defiance of threat of violent death and legal sanctions.[1]

Since the Overhill Cherokees held a traditional place of leadership in the tribe, their reactions both to the pressure on their lands and to the war would be watched by the tribesmen at large as well as by the colonials. Indeed when the Overhills considered their own accumulated grievances with the colonies as well as the rebellion against the king, it seemed logical that they should be actively pro-British. But their friend John Stuart, the British Indian superintendent in the South, thought otherwise, for he wanted the Cherokees to remain inactive until they could be used as auxiliaries in conjunction with troops. He was afraid that they would kill rebel and Loyalist alike. His policy in 1775–1776 then was to keep the southern tribes loyal and ready to act when called upon.[2] But the Cherokees were impatient, angry, and aggravated in the extreme. The long history of abuses by the Virginians (as all southern frontiersmen were called) alone justified action, but if that were not enough, they were displeased that the colonials had abused John Stuart and Alexander Cameron, the principal Cherokee deputy in the Indian department, and, worse yet, the Americans had reduced the trade to a mere trickle of goods.

In large measure the dilemma faced by the southern tribes in 1775–1776 is more than epitomized in the predicament of the Cherokees who seemed damned if they did and damned if they did not. If they did try to drive the settlers out of the mountains, they would risk both the anger of Stuart and the retaliation of the Americans, while if they did not strike, the Americans would continue advancing. The councils of the Cherokees were long and troubled in the winter of 1775–1776. A group of young men under the leadership of Dragging Canoe (who had gained some fame already at the Transylvania purchase by warning that the land would prove "dark and bloody") insisted that tribal leadership was lacking, that the principal chiefs had grown "too old to hunt," and that the young men should lead the nation to honor by driving out the settlers. By April of 1776 the council fires burned almost constantly. To the beloved town of Chota journeyed the leaders of the towns, including Dragging Canoe and his followers, the British agent Alexander Cameron, and, as the superintendent's personal representative, his brother Henry Stuart, who arrived in April with fifteen hundred pounds of powder.[3]

Dragging Canoe urged war; the Raven, the Great Warrior, and the Little Carpenter proposed patience, discussion, and deliberation; the Englishmen requested patient vigilance. But the war faction became so persuasive that finally Cameron and Stuart despaired and sought a chance to mediate with the settlers in the hope that they could forestall war. Their position, although they could hardly state it publicly, was that action in the spring before British troops arrived below the Chesapeake held little hope of success, for both frontier and tidewater would be alarmed, and Indian attacks would thereby profit the Patriots who could scream "villainy" and persuade the undecided that the American cause was more noble. The two agents did not reckon with frontier guile, however, for when their letters warning of impending attack if the settlers did not withdraw were received, the frontiersmen redrafted these and recast them as warnings for the king's friends only.[4] The Cherokees were infuriated by this treachery and by the obvious fact that the frontiersmen were making no preparations to move but were gathering the people into the blockhouses. As a result the war faction completely prevailed and were much pleased therefore when a group of northern tribesmen appeared in early May to report that they also were preparing for war.[5]

During May the Cherokees laid their plans; in June they took action. First the Lower Town warriors advanced, carrying axe and torch into the backcountry of South Carolina and Georgia. Within a month the North Carolina settlements as well as the outposts at Watauga and Holston had been attacked.

The most immediate effect of the Cherokee attacks was to arouse the frontier, sending a thrill of alarm across the four southern colonies. For the Cherokees there was satisfaction that the encroachments of the frontier folk had stopped for a time. Many families had retreated to safer districts. But quickly Patriot militia captains mustered their forces, state governments cried out against British treachery, and plans were laid for punitive expeditions. In South Carolina the alarm was more strident because Charleston was under British attack. To the minds of colonials accustomed to think in terms of British conspiracy, the coincidence of the Indian attacks and the coastal assault seemed all of a piece, a plot launched by the royal military command. It is true that Superintendent Stuart had visited General Clinton at Cape Fear in early May but no arrangements were made. Patriot leaders believed, however, that the plans laid had called for the Cherokee actions in conjunction with the British strike which would then be followed by a Creek attack.[6]

The Creeks, however, were still in a period of uncertainty. The British asked them to stand firm, while, among the Lower Creek towns, American agents led by George Galphin preached neutrality. Also there was Georgia's somewhat confused Indian policy. While on the one hand Sir James Wright, the royal governor, and the Patriot leaders competed with one another, on the other hand they cooperated in Indian affairs, for neither party wanted war with the Creeks.[7] But to the Creeks, most Georgians appeared no different from the other land-hungry colonials. Along the Georgia frontier the settlers schemed to grab the tribal lands, even at times provoking the Creeks in hope of a war for which the frontiersmen could retaliate and gain satisfaction by more demands for land. Thus the Creeks heard assurances from the British that all would be well if they supported the king, blandishments from the Americans urging neutrality, and at the same time threats from colonials eager for land.

While the tribal leaders had reason for resentment, nevertheless the cabins of the settlers had not pushed so far into Creek territory as onto Cherokee lands. Other problems also stood in the way of Creek assistance to the British. For a number of years there had been a war with the Choctaws, a war which the British supplied and at times fomented on the ancient principle of divide and conquer. But if the British now wished their assistance or that of the Choctaws, British policy would have to change. Early on, then, the Creeks urged that peace be made between the two tribes. In addition to the Choctaw problem the Creeks worried over supplies for their warriors and also about reports circulated that a detachment of British troops would be moved through the Creek country against the South Carolina frontier. Supplies they would welcome in their villages, soldiers they would not.[8]

Having no immediate and pressing reason to attack the colonials as did the Cherokees, the Creeks had adopted a wait-and-see attitude through the first six months of 1776. Then came word of the Cherokee attacks and requests for aid from their brethren. Reluctant still the Creeks asked the advice of John Stuart, who as of August was still advising neutrality. Then the superintendent got firsthand reports that the Cherokees had to be supported or they would be crushed by the Patriots. Accordingly he asked the Creeks to move against the frontier, but the Creeks by then knew more of what was happening in the Cherokee country than did Stuart or his deputies.[9] The refugees from the Cherokee towns had come with tales of destruction by the Patriot armies.

What drove the Cherokees south were the expeditions organized by the four southern states. Within two weeks after the first Cherokee attack against South Carolina the militia was being rallied, although everything in the state was rather confused because of the double alarm in what appeared to be simultaneous attacks from east and west. It was therefore some weeks before the Cherokee Lower Towns were attacked, but when the troops from South Carolina came they struck with a vengeance, levelling most of those villages.[10]

In the meantime North Carolina forces had marched to the frontier where they waited for supplies and then crossed into the mountains headed for the Cherokee Middle settlements.[11] Most of the Cherokees wisely had melted away into the mountains, leaving behind empty villages which the Americans put to the torch. Beyond the mountains the Overhills were still untouched but there was a Virginia expedition gathering. In the Overhill towns there was much discussion over the proper course of action. Dragging Canoe wanted to lie in wait for the Patriots at an advantageous spot, perhaps at a river crossing, and give battle. But the chiefs who argued for strategic withdrawal and application for a truce prevailed. No band of fifteen hundred warriors, however courageous, could stand the fire of five or six thousand Americans.[12]

Early in October the Virginians crossed the Holston and marched toward the heart of the Overhill country and the beloved town of Chota. After the Virginia army crossed the French Broad they met messengers who came in under a sign of truce asking for a cease-fire. By November a truce was granted, but this was too late to save many villages and the thousands of bushels of corn and potatoes cached for winter provisions.[13]

Now the Cherokees faced a bleak winter and a dismal spring. From north, east, and south their enemies had come to lay waste to their towns, and as the tribal leaders guessed, the treaty conferences proposed for the spring would mean demands for more land, a prospect not pleasing to the Cherokees. In May of 1777 the Lower and Middle town representatives journeyed to Dewitt's Corner, South Carolina, where they agreed to peace and of course a land cession. Two months later at the Long Island of the Holston River the Overhill Cherokee reached a similar settlement. The first of a long series of penalties forced on the Cherokees by the new nation was now being exacted.[14]

The fate of the Cherokees was a lesson not lost on the Creeks. Through the winter of 1776–1777 they had exchanged messages with John Stuart about attacking the Georgia and South Carolina frontier, but they committed themselves only on the condition of constant assistance in the form of supplies from Stuart and the mediation of a peace with the Choctaws.[15]

The Choctaws, alas, had problems enough that the Creeks need not fear warfare. In the spring of 1777 visitors to the Choctaw villages found a woeful scene. Excessive drinking was decimating the nation, for rum literally flowed into every town. The sober chiefs cried out for relief, for rum came in not

only by the bottle but also by the keg and barrel. The British
traders from Pensacola and Mobile kept the Choctaws in a
state of intoxication. By one account women sat weeping over
the unconscious forms of their husbands lying in the streets.
Charles Stuart said the passion for rum was alcoholic: "It [rum]
is like a woman—when a man wanted her and saw her—He
must have her!"[16]

As much as anything else then, if the British wished the
help of the Choctaws they had to try to plug the cask. This
would have to be taken up at the meeting of the Choctaws
and the Chickasaws scheduled for Mobile in May of 1777.
Even then care would have to be taken for on such occasions
it was expected that some rum would be distributed. In Mobile
the superintendent heard the Choctaws promise peace and
assistance for the Mississippi river patrol, but their strongest
words, indeed their pleas, were requests that the rum be cur-
tailed. John Stuart assured the Choctaws of his good intentions, but when he returned to Pensacola he found that the
royal governor, Peter Chester, listened to traders more than to
the superintendent, so the rum continued to flow.[17]

As a result of the Mobile conference the Creek-Choctaw
War was brought to a close. Choctaw parties could now aid in
scouting the Mississippi River for American expeditions, while
the Creeks could prepare for an assault against the colonies.
Many of the Creeks in the meantime had been persuaded to
move east against the settlements once the crops were gathered.
One part of the tribe, however, was meeting with the Patriots
in the summer of 1777. They were urged to drive the British
Creek deputy, David Taitt, and Alexander Cameron, tempo-
rarily in the Creek country, out of the Creek towns. Upon
leaving the Americans, a group of these Lower Creeks, filled
with "rum and good words" moved west with the intention
not just of driving Taitt and Cameron away but of killing
them. But if the rum made them daring it also made them
talkative, and Alexander McGillivray, the assistant British
commissary in the Upper Creek towns, learned of the plot
and warned Taitt and Cameron. When the two Englishmen

eluded them, the Lower Creeks chased the pro-British traders out so that by December of 1777 the Creek towns were empty of British representatives and traders.[18]

During the winter of 1777–1778 a major policy change in overall war strategy was undertaken by the British command, a change which would directly involve the southern Indians.[19] Foiled in their plans to stamp out rebellion by isolating New England, the British leaders decided to move the major theater of operations south of the Chesapeake, where the Indians and Loyalists could be of aid in restoring the colonies. According to the official orders issued from London in March, the southern Indian warriors were to be brought to the frontier of Georgia and South Carolina where they could strike at the same time that a British expedition attacked Savannah.

Accordingly the Cherokees and the Creeks were approached by officials of the British Indian department and were asked to prepare for war. Unfortunately the Creeks were finding it difficult to unite because of the strong pro-American faction among the Lower Creeks plus the fact that the governor of East Florida regarded the Seminole Creeks as his personal troops, an attitude which infuriated John Stuart.[20] Thus Stuart could count on only the Upper Creeks where he had the assistance of David Taitt and the rising influence of Alexander McGillivray, the assistant commissary, whose blood connections in the tribe made him politically powerful.

The Cherokees on the other hand continued to make pledges of affection but they had not yet recovered from the war of 1776 or the treaties of 1777.[21] Goods promised had not been delivered, the boundary agreed upon had not been surveyed, and the frontiersmen still took up tribal lands at will. The Cherokee simply were not ready to make war in 1778.

When the British invasion of Georgia came in late 1778 one of the first moves made by the British was to send a column inland toward Augusta to meet the Indians under John Stuart and to rally the Loyalists.[22] When the British reached Augusta the commander was dismayed. Where were the numerous friends of the king so long described by the exiles as being in

the majority in the backcountry? Few Loyalists emerged and
no Indians were to be seen. In a rage the British officer led
his men away toward Savannah.

Indeed where were the forest warriors and their British
friends at the time the column was in Augusta? They were
busy with life as usual, waiting for the word to come from
Stuart. The failure was not of design or intention but a matter
of communication. Messages to inform John Stuart were not
sent until after the British landing so that it was late January
before the word reached Pensacola. As soon as the dispatches
came, Stuart sent word to the Creeks, but even so it was early
March before about four hundred Creek warriors and fifty de-
partmental officials and Loyalist traders reached the Ogeechee
to wait for the expected British force. They were two months
too late. Soon troops did approach but they were American,
not British. The Creek leaders protested that they had no intention of doing battle without the aid of the king's troops.
The majority of the Creeks thus went home, while a few
joined Alexander McGillivray in slipping through the Patriot
lines to reach the British at Savannah. There they served as
raiders for some weeks before returning home.[23]

If the Creeks were frustrated in their attempts to help crush
the colonial rebellion so were the other tribes in the South.[24]
Some Choctaw had patrolled the Mississippi, but when they
relaxed their watch early in 1778 a party of Americans slipped
past to raid the settlements at Natchez and Manchac and reach
New Orleans. In the Cherokee country the failure of the tribe
to aid the British aroused bitter feelings within the tribe. For
this and other reasons Dragging Canoe and his followers emigrated southward to establish new towns which would come
to be known as the Chickamauga Cherokee villages. In those
villages the British agents moved freely and in the winter of
1778–1779 the Chickamaugas were persuaded to prepare for
action with the coming of spring. When the warriors moved
away in April a raiding party from the Virginia overmountain
settlements came south and destroyed their towns. After re-
building their dwellings, the Chickamaugas went back toward

the frontier only to be met by a large force of South Carolinians who chased them back once more.

The years 1778 and 1779 were not fruitful for the southern tribes in their efforts to aid the British in crushing the colonial rebellion. Disappointed also were John Stuart and certain members of Parliament, particularly those among the opposition to the war, who questioned spending thousands of pounds sterling on Indian affairs without visible results.[25]

But for John Stuart the frustrations and labors of public office came to an end in March 1779, when he died in Pensacola after a tedious and painful illness.[26] The southern Indians had reason to mourn, for they had lost a powerful advocate and a man who grasped something of the predicament in which the tribes were placed as the colonials pressed against them. With Stuart gone there was no one who could argue effectively with the officials in London over treatment of the tribes. Although Stuart was perhaps never so influential as Sir William Johnson in the North, he did have the respect of the southern Indians.

In addition to the changes which would come in Indian affairs as a result of Stuart's death, there were also the shifts taking place in the military conflict. After 1779 the Spanish moved against British outposts on the Mississippi and the Gulf, which made it imperative to call on the Creeks, Chickasaws, and Choctaws.[27]

In 1780 Mobile fell but Pensacola held out until a relief fleet came, a success credited in part to the presence of nearly two thousand Creek warriors led by Alexander McGillivray and William McIntosh. When the Spanish expedition arrived, the Spanish commander was unhappy about the odds and sought to reduce them by accusing the British of using uncivilized barbarians in warfare against the army of a Christian prince. The British commander informed his adversary that he would defend his post with whatever means at his disposal. On that occasion the Spanish chose to wait and when a British relief fleet appeared, the dons withdrew. In letters to Alexander McGillivray, Brig. Gen. John Campbell, the commandant at Pensacola, was fulsome in thanking the Creeks for their aid, crediting them with saving the post.[28]

While the Creeks served at Pensacola, some Cherokees had gone to the assistance of the British outpost at Augusta.[29] The commander there was Thomas Brown, a Loyalist from South Carolina who had fled to East Florida, joined the East Florida Rangers, gotten into the good graces of Gov. Patrick Tonyn, and now was not only the commander of the British outpost at Augusta but also the superintendent of the newly created Atlantic Division of the Southern Indian Department. (This division had been decided upon after the death of Stuart, with Brown given the Atlantic Division and Alexander Cameron, to his great dismay, the Mississippi Division.) The Patriots had been drawn to Augusta in part by the supplies cached there for conferences with the Cherokees and Creeks. After some weeks of siege a British rescue force arrived and the Americans had to withdraw.

The Cherokees who fought with the superintendent at Augusta reflected the tribe's first steps at renewing their support of the British against the Americans. Four years had passed since the conflict of 1776, and the painful memories had dimmed. In addition the British has succeeded in recovering Georgia and South Carolina, and so the Cherokees reasoned that the presence of royal troops in the South would give them protection. Of course the encroachment of their land by the frontiersmen had never stopped. The warriors who came home from Augusta loaded with goods and covered in glory now urged their comrades to act upon Thomas Brown's request that the tribe attack the frontiers once again.

There were however few secrets in the Cherokee country. Patriot traders soon passed word of the proposed raids and when some warriors started out against the South Carolina frontier in the fall of 1780 their action provided an excuse for the frontiersmen to strike. Down the Holston came the Patriots raiding and burning villages. Although the destruction was by no means as systematic as it had been in 1776, a number of towns were burned including the principal Overhill town of Chota.[30]

It was evident from these raids to many Cherokee leaders that their towns now lay so close to the frontiersmen and so open to punitive expeditions that the course of accommodation was the most sensible. Reports of these intentions reached the Virginia frontier early in 1781. Accordingly, one of the frontier leaders suggested that the commander of the Continental forces in the South, Gen. Nathaniel Greene, use this opportunity to seek some permanent settlement with the tribe, for by Patriot definition the Cherokees had broken the treaty of 1777 and by Cherokee definition the treaty had never been fulfilled.[31] A new treaty would give the Cherokees temporary security against renewed warfare and give the frontiersmen freedom to oppose the British army in the South. Of course the Cherokees were not willing to give up all hope of British aid so that at the same time that the word went to the Virginia frontier, talks promised the aid of the tribe to the British in any new offensive. Cherokee motives seem clear. They were unwilling to see the door closed to cooperation with the British if for some reason Patriot resistance collapsed and British control was restored.[32]

There seemed little likelihood, however, that the British would recover the colonies. Everywhere in the South British arms were pressed by their adversaries. In the Southwest the Spanish had taken Mobile, attacked Pensacola once, and were preparing for a second and successful siege. The Choctaws and Creeks had become disgusted with the inconsistent policy of General Campbell and would no longer rally at his call. Like the proverbial shepherd Campbell found that when his enemy did actually materialize there were very few Choctaws and Creeks present. With the fall of Pensacola the Gulf coast was closed to British communication with the Creeks, Choctaws, and Chickasaws.[33]

Now the messengers would have to move overland along the old trading paths to Augusta where Thomas Brown was located and where Alexander Cameron headed after the fall of Pensacola. But soon this post was no longer in British hands either, for the Patriots overwhelmed Augusta in the spring of 1781 and the British were soon reduced to the environs of

Charleston and Savannah.[34] Even then the southern tribes tried to get through to the British. In the course of one such cross-country expedition, the principal warrior of the Upper Creeks, Emistisiguo, was killed, leaving a power vacuum that would be filled by Alexander McGillivray, now fully committed to life with his mother's people.[35]

By the end of 1781 the southern tribes were faced with hard choices. They remained essentially where they were at the beginning of the war though they had lost some lands by cession during the war. Their British allies had been driven away from the Gulf and now held two enclaves on the southern coast (plus of course East Florida). Communication with either Charleston or Savannah became impossible so that tribal representatives would have to travel the paths to Saint Augustine if they chose to remain loyal to the British.

On the other hand there was the option of making peace with the Americans, the choice eventually taken by the Cherokees and the Chickasaws.[36] The Choctaws wavered, but the Creeks remained firm. Then in 1782 they were slapped with the news that the British were evacuating the Floridas. Some chiefs would not believe it: they protested that it was a Virginia lie; others demanded to be taken along in the British ships. Eventually they faced the hard reality, and led by Alexander McGillivray the tribe sought a marriage of convenience with the Spanish.[37]

No matter what each tribe chose at war's end, they all faced the same American demand. The Patriots looked upon the southern Indians as the defeated allies of the British, who, as conquered enemies should give up the spoils of war, in this case land. The Patriot attitude is summed up well in the outlook of the North Carolina legislature, which seems to have been struck by an epidemic of land fever. By rights, said the North Carolinians, we now own *all* the Cherokee lands, but out of our generosity the Cherokees may live on them until we can provide a reservation for the tribe.[38]

The policy and attitude assumed by the states during and just after the war thus becomes the basis for federal policy and attitude to a large degree. The defeated enemy should never be allowed to forget, their land should become part of the public domain. The demand for Indian land, indeed, would never cease. If the American Revolution was a time of national beginnings in politics and society, it was equally so in Indian policy, for with the nation's beginnings emerged the ideas of displacement and removal, ideas which came to fruition in the nineteenth century and have not died in the present century.

NOTES

1. Thomas P. Abernethy, *From Frontier to Plantation in Tennessee*, (Memphis, Tenn.: Memphis State Press, 1955), chap. 9 and 12; Louis DeVorsey, Jr., *The Indian Boundary in the Southern Colonies, 1763–1775* (Chapel Hill: University of North Carolina Press, 1966), chap. 2; and Jack M. Sosin, *The Revolutionary Frontier, 1763–1783* (New York: Holt, Rinehart and Winston, 1967), chap. 4 and 5.

2. Philip M. Hamer, "John Stuart's Indian Policy during the Early Months of the American Revolution," *Mississippi Valley Historical Review* 17 (1930–1931): 351–366; idem, "The Wataugans and the Cherokee Indians in 1776," *East Tennessee Historical Society Publications* 3 (1931): 108–126.

3. Henry Stuart to John Stuart, 7 May 1776, British Public Record Office, Colonial Office Papers, series 5 (Film from the Library of Congress), 77: 145; same to the same, August 1776, in William L. Saunders, ed., *The Colonial Records of North Carolina*, 14 vols. (Raleigh; 1886–1890), 10: 763–785. The British Public Record Office papers are hereafter cited CO5, vol.: page.

4. Henry Stuart and Alexander Cameron to the Wataugans, 7 May 1776, CO5, 77: 143; John Carter to Cameron and Stuart, 13 May 1776, ibid., p. 149; Saunders, Report of Isaac Thomas, n.d., *Colonial Records*, 10: 769; and Henry Stuart to Edward Wilkinson, 28 June 1776, CO5, 77: 156.

5. Henry Stuart to John Stuart, August 1776, CO5, 77: 145ff.

6. John Stuart to Henry Clinton, 9 May 1776, CO5, 77: 111; Frederick Mulcaster to Clinton, 16 April 1776, Clinton Papers, William L. Clements Library, University of Michigan; John Stuart to Henry Clinton, 8 May 1776, Clinton Papers, Clements Library. For contemporary opinion in South Carolina about the existence of a plot see Henry Laurens to John Laurens, 14 August 1776, in Henry Laurens, *A South Carolina Protest against Slavery* (New York, 1861), pp. 26–27, and in David Ramsay, *The Revolution of South Carolina from a British Province to an Independent State*, 2 vols. (Trenton, N.J., 1785), 1: 334–335.

7. Sir James Wright to Lord Dartmouth, 20 June 1775, in G. W. J. De-Renne, ed., "Letters from Governor Sir James Wright to the Earl of Dartmouth and Lord George Germain, Secretaries of State for America, from August 24, 1774, to February 17, 1782," *Collections of the Georgia Historical Society* 3 (1873): 189–190; Council held at the Governor's

House, 31 October 1775, in Lilla M. Hawes, "Proceedings and Minutes of the Governor and Council of Georgia, October 4, 1774, through November 7, 1775, and September 6, 1779, through September 20, 1780," *Georgia Historical Quarterly* 34 (1950): 208–226, 288–312; ibid. 35 (1951): 31–59, 126–151, 196–221. Information on Creek affairs before 1775 may be found in David Corkran, *The Creek Frontier, 1540–1783* (Norman: University of Oklahoma Press, 1967).

8. David Taitt to John Stuart, 1 August 1775, CO5, 76: 177; talk of John Stuart to the Creeks, 15 August 1775, CO5, 76: 181.

9. Talk of Emistisiguo to John Stuart, 19 November 1776, CO5, 78: 81; John Stuart to Lord George Germain, 24 November 1776, CO5, 78: 72.

10. Journal of an Expedition in 1776 against the Cherokees under the Command of Captain Peter Clinton, Lyman C. Draper Collections, Wisconsin State Historical Society (microfilm), Thomas Sumter Papers, 3: 164–175; Andrew Williamson to Griffith Rutherford, 14 August 1776, Saunders, *Colonial Records*, 10: 745–748; same to William H. Drayton, 22 August 1776, in R. W. Gibbes, ed., *Documentary History of the American Revolution, 1774–1782*, 3 vols. (New York, 1853–1857), 2: 32.

11. Griffith Rutherford to the North Carolina Council, 1 September 1776, Saunders, *Colonial Records*, 10: 788–789; William Lenoir, "Journal of the Cherokee Expedition, 1776," *Journal of Southern History* 6 (1940): 247–249.

12. William Christian to Patrick Henry, 27 October 1776, "Revolutionary Correspondence," *Virginia Magazine of History and Biography* 17 (1908): 61–64, 170–173.

13. Ibid.; Captain Joseph Martin's Orderly Book of the Cherokee Expedition, Draper Collections, Virginia Papers, 8: 72–73; *Virginia Gazette* (Purdie's), 29 November 1776, p. 2.

14. Proceedings of the Virginia Commissioners with the Cherokee, April 1777, Draper Collections, Preston Papers, 4: 122–149; Treaty of Dewitt's Corner, John Steele Papers, 1777–1779, Southern Historical Collections, University of North Carolina; Archibald Henderson, "The Treaty of Long Island of Holston," *North Carolina Historical Review* 8 (1931): 55–116.

15. John Stuart to George Germain, 10 March 1777, CO5, 78: 105.

16. Charles Stuart to John Stuart, 4 March 1777, CO5, 78: 126; Charles Stuart's Report of his visit to the Choctaw Country, 1 July 1778, CO5, 79: 196–202.

17. John Stuart to Germain, 14 June 1777, CO5, 78: 143; William Howe to Stuart, 12 July 1777, CO5, 94: 401; Meeting of Chester, Stiell, and Stuart (concerning trade and rum), 10 April 1777, CO5, 78: 157.

18. Alexander McGillivray to John Stuart, 21 September 1777, CO5, 79: 33; John Stuart to George Germain, 6 October 1777, ibid., p. 29.

19. George Germain to Henry Clinton, 8 March 1778, in Benjamin F. Stevens, ed., *Facsimiles of Manuscripts in European Archives Relating to America, 1773–1783*, 25 vols. (London, 1890), 11; no. 1062; same to Stuart, 5 November 1777, CO5, 78: 180; and Paul H. Smith, *Loyalists and Redcoats: A Study in British Revolutionary Policy* (Chapel Hill, N.C.: Institute of Early American History and Culture, 1964), chap. 6.

20. Patrick Tonyn to Henry Clinton, 8 June 1776, CO5, 556: 683–688; same to Germain, 29 April 1778, CO5, 558: 279; John Stuart to Tonyn,

10 July 1778, ibid., p. 451; same to Germain, 23 February 1777, ibid., pp. 19–22; and same to the same, 19 May 1778, ibid., p. 160.

21. Talks from the Cherokee to LeRoy Hammond and Edward Wilkinson, 26 September 1778, Laurens Papers, Bundle 46, South Carolina Historical Society.

22. Augustin Prevost to David Taitt, 14 March 1779, CO5, 80: 246; Archibald Campbell to the Creeks (1779), Clinton Papers, William L. Clements Library.

23. John Stuart to David Taitt, 1 February 1779, CO5, 80: 158; Taitt to Germain, 6 August 1779, ibid., p. 234; Andrew Williamson to Benjamin Lincoln, 19 January 1779, Andrew Williamson Papers, South Carolina Library, University of South Carolina; James Keef to David Holms, 27 April 1779, CO5, 80: 205.

24. Hardy Perry to Farquhar Bethune, 4 February 1778, CO5, 79: 116; John W. Caughey, "Willing's Raid Down the Mississippi," *Louisiana Historical Quarterly* 15 (1932): 5–36; William Thompson to Cameron, 14 November 1776, CO5, 94: 157; Walter Scott to Cameron, 27 March 1779, CO5, 80: 179; Henry Hamilton to Stuart, 25 December 1778, CO5, 597: pt. 1, 121; Patrick Henry to Richard Caswell, 8 January 1779, Richard Caswell Papers, North Carolina Department of Archives and History; Cameron to Germain, 10 May 1779, CO5, 80: 171; *Gazette of the State of South Carolina*, 24 September 1779, p. 2.

25. John Almon, ed., *The Parliamentary Register; or, History of the Proceedings and Debates of the House of Commons*, 17 vols. (London, 1775–1780), 12: 255, 257, 258ff; Germain to Stuart, 3 March 1779, CO5, 81: 18; Murray S. Downs, "British Parliamentary Opinion and American Independence, 1776–1783," paper given at the Thirteenth Conference on Early American History, Columbia, S. C., March 1962.

26. Alexander Cameron and Charles Stuart to George Germain, 26 March 1779, CO5, 80: 109.

27. John R. Alden, *The American Revolution, 1775–1783* (New York: Harper and Row, 1962).

28. Extract of a letter from William McIntosh, 20 March 1780, CO5, 81: 167; Alexander McGillivray to Thomas Brown, 25 March 1780, ibid., p. 169; same to same, 13 May 1780, ibid., p. 240; John Campbell to Thomas, 15 November 1780, Clinton Papers, William L. Clements Library; same to McGillivray, 22 November 1780, CO5, 82: 451.

29. Charles Shaw to George Germain, 18 September 1780, CO5, 82: 318; *Royal Gazette of South Carolina*, 27 September 1780, ibid., p. 2.

30. Thomas Brown to Cornwallis, 17 December 1780, Clinton Papers, Clements Library; Joseph Martin to Thomas Jefferson, 12 December 1780, Draper Collections, Tennessee Papers, 1: 41; Arthur Campbell to Thomas Jefferson, 15 January 1781, William P. Palmer et al., *Calendar of Virginia State Papers and Other Manuscripts, 1652-1781*, 11 vols. (Richmond, 1875–1893), 1: 434–437. Much to his surprise Colonel Campbell found in a chief's baggage "which he left behind in his fight, various manuscripts, Copies of Treaties, Letters, and other Archives of the nation, some which shews the double game that people has been carrying on during the present war." Among the papers are included a copy of the King's Proclamation of 1763 and the Great Warrior's certificate of membership in the St. Andrew's Society of Charleston, S.C., dated 30 November 1773. In con-

nection with this unique collection see John R. Alden, "The Eighteenth-Century Cherokee Archives," *American Archivist* 5 (1942) : 240–244.

31. Arthur Campbell to Nathanael Greene, 8 February 1781, Nathanael Greene Letterbook, Library of Congress; same to Jefferson, 27 January 1781, Palmer, *State Papers*, 1: 464–465.

32. Thomas Brown to Cornwallis, 17 December 1780, Clinton Papers, William L. Clements Library; A Talk from the Cherokee Nation Delivered by the Raven of Chota at Savannah, 1 September 1781, CO5, 82: 287.

33. Talk of Frenchumastabie, Great Medal chief of the Choctaw, to Alexander Cameron, 1 April 1781, CO5, 82: 210; *Royal Gazette of South Carolina*, 12 May 1781, p. 2; John W. Caughey, *Bernardo de Galvez in Louisiana, 1776–1783* (Berkeley: University of California, 1934) , chaps. 11 and 12.

34. Thomas Brown to Germain, 9 August 1781, CO5, 82: 252; Cameron to Germain, 27 May 1781, ibid., p. 204 .

35. Anthony Wayne to Nathanael Greene, 24 June 1782, Papers of the Continental Congress (National Archives) , no. 155, 2: 491–495; James H. O'Donnell III, "Alexander McGillivray: Training for Leadership, 1777–1783," *Georgia Historical Quarterly* 49 (1965) : 172–186.

36. A Talk from us (Poymace Tauhaw, Mingo Homaw, Tuskau Pulasso, and Paymingo) to be delivered by Mr. Simon Burney to the Commanders of every different Station between this Nation and the falls of the Ohio River, 9 July 1782, Draper Collections, Tennessee Papers, 1: 50; A Message sent to the middle Grounds by Charles Beaman a half breed & by a fellow called the Horn to the Vallies (by General Andrew Pickens) , 25 September 1782, Force Transcripts, Georgia Records, Library of Congress; A Talk delivered by General Pickens to the Head Men of the Cherokee Nation, 17 October 1782, ibid.; A Talk to Colonel Joseph Martin by Old Tassel, 25 September 1782, Saunders, *Colonial Records*, 16: 415–416; William Christian to Benjamin Harrison, 15 December 1782, Palmer, *State Papers*, 3: 398.

37. John W. Caughey, *McGillivray of the Creeks* (Norman: University of Oklahoma, 1938) , pp. 22–26.

38. Alexander Martin to the Cherokees, 25 May 1783, Saunders, *Colonial Records*, 14: 810; *Laws . . . relating to Indians and Indian affairs, from 1633 to 1831 . . .* (Washington, 1832) , pp. 170–171.

SOURCES CITED

Primary Sources

Almon, John, ed. *The Parliamentary Register; or, History of the Proceedings and Debates of the House of Commons.* 17 vols. London, 1775–1780.

British Public Record Office. Colonial Office Papers, series 5.

Caswell, Richard. Richard Caswell Papers. North Carolina Department of Archives and History.

Clinton, Henry. Sir Henry Clinton Papers. William L. Clements Library, University of Michigan. Ann Arbor, Michigan.

Draper, Lyman C. Lyman C. Draper Collections. Wisconsin State Historical Society. Madison, Wisconsin.

Force, Peter. Force Transcripts of Georgia Records. Library of Congress. Washington, D.C.

Gazette of the State of South Carolina. Charleston, S.C.

Gibbes, R. W., ed. *Documentary History of the American Revolution, 1774–1782.* 3 vols. New York, 1853–1857.

Hawes, Lilla M., ed. "Proceedings and Minutes of the Governor and Council of Georgia, October 4, 1774, through November 7, 1775, and September 6, 1779, through September 20, 1780." *Georgia Historical Quarterly* 35 (1950). 208–226, 288–312; ibid., 35 (1951) : 31–59, 126–151, 196–221.

Laurens, Henry. Henry Laurens Papers. South Carolina Historical Society. Charleston, S.C.

———. *A South Carolina Protest Against Slavery,* New York, 1861.

Laws . . . Relating to Indian and Indian Affairs, from 1633 to 1831 . . . . Washington, 1832.

Lenoir, William. "Journal of the Cherokee Expedition, 1776." *Journal of Southern History* 6 (1940) : 247–249.

Palmer, William P., et al. *Calendar of Virginia State Papers and Other Manuscripts, 1652–1781.* 11 vols. Richmond, 1785–1893.

Papers of the Continental Congress. National Archives. Washington, D.C.

"Revolutionary Correspondence." *Virginia Magazine of History and Biography* 17 (1908) : 61–64, 170–173

Royal Gazette of South Carolina. Charleston, S.C.

Saunders, William. L., ed. *The Colonial Records of North Carolina.* 14 vols. Raleigh, N.C., 1886–1890.

Steele, John. John Steele Papers. Southern Historical Collections. University of North Carolina. Chapel Hill, N.C.

Stevens, Benjamin F., ed. *Facsimiles of Manuscripts in European Archives Relating to America, 1773–1783.* 25 vols. London, 1890.

Williamson, Andrew. Andrew Williamson Papers. South Caroliniana Library. University of South Carolina. Columbia, S.C.

Wright, James. "Letters from Governor Sir James Wright to the Earl of Dartmouth and Lord George Germain, Secretaries of State for America, from August 24, 1774, to February 17, 1782. *"Collections of the Georgia Historical Society* 3 (1873) : 189–190.

Secondary Sources

Abernethy, Thomas P. *From Frontier to Plantation in Tennessee.* Memphis: Memphis State Press, 1955.

Alden, John R. *The American Revolution, 1775–1783.* New York: Harper and Row, 1962.

———. "The Eighteenth-Century Cherokees Archives." *American Archivist* 5 (1942) : 240–244.

Caughey, John W. *Bernardo de Galvez in Louisiana, 1776–1783.* Berkeley: University of California, 1934.

———. *McGillivray of the Creeks.* Norman: University of Oklahoma Press. 1938.

———. "Willing's Raid Down the Mississippi." *Louisiana Historical Quarterly* 15 (1932) : 5–36.

Corkran, David H. *The Creek Frontier, 1540–1783.* Norman: University of Oklahoma Press, 1967.

DeVorsey, Louis, Jr. *The Indian Boundary in the Southern Colonies, 1763–1775.* Chapel Hill: University of North Carolina Press, 1966.

Downs, Murray S. "British Parliamentary Opinion and American Independence, 1776–1783." Thirteenth Conference on Early American History, Columbia, S.C., March 1962.

Hamer, Philip M. "John Stuart's Indian Policy during the Early Months of the American Revolution." *Mississippi Valley Historical Review* 17 (1930–1931): 351–366.

———. "The Wataugans and the Cherokee Indians in 1776." *East Tennessee Historical Society* Publications 3 (1931): 108–126.

Henderson, Archibald. "The Treaty of Long Island of Holston." *North Carolina Historical Review* 8 (1931): 55–116.

O'Donnell, James H., III. "Alexander McGillivray: Training for Leadership, 1777–1783." *Georgia Historical Quarterly* 49 (1965): 172–186.

Ramsay, David. *The Revolution of South Carolina from a British Province to an Independent State.* 2 vols. Trenton, N.J., 1785.

Smith, Paul. *Loyalists and Redcoats: A Study in British Revolutionary Policy.* Chapel Hill, N.C.: Institute of Early American History and Culture, 1964.

Sosin, Jack M. *The Revolutionary Frontier, 1763–1783.* New York: Holt, Rinehart and Winston, 1967.

Spanish Policy
toward the Southern Indians
in the 1790s

Jack D. L. Holmes

The Cold War is really not confined to recent American history. During the 1790s the United States and Spain vied for control over the "uncommitted Nations," a role played at that time by the fifty thousand Choctaws, Chickasaws, Cherokees, and Creeks. R. S. Cotterill, noting the importance of these Indian tribes, says, "Facing the Americans on the north and east, they were at the same time a threat to the southern frontier and a barrier to southern expansion."[1] Spain's policy, in its broadest sense, aimed at alliances with these tribes to check the vigorous expansion of American settlers and land speculators.

Spanish governors appreciated the value of such Indian allies. Gov. Vicente Manuel de Zéspedes wrote from Saint Augustine that the Indians should be supplied with arms and ammunition for hunting and for protection against English or American interlopers.[2] From Pensacola, Gov. Arturo O'Neill wrote that by giving the Indians presents, he had won their loyalty and was able to make use of Indians "to spread terror on the frontiers of Georgia and Carolina" should circumstances require such hostility.[3] Govs. Bernardo de Gálvez and Esteban Miró suggested in 1786 that Spain secretly give the Indians quantities of arms and munitions so that they might check the American advance.[4]

Spanish policy was modified during the final decade of the

eighteenth century as the United States, French Jacobins, and English agents posed threats to the security of the Spanish-American frontier. Two Spanish officials were primarily responsible for drafting and executing this policy—Gayoso and Carondelet. Manuel Gayoso de Lemos became the first governor of the Natchez District in 1789 at a time when the South Carolina Yazoo Company sought to open Spanish lands along the Mississippi River to land speculators.[5] Gov. gen. Francisco Luis Héctor, Baron de Carondelet, had come to New Orleans in December 1791 from a successful term as governor and intendant of several colonies in the kingdom of Guatemala. His Indian policy there was crowned with success, but he faced different challenges in Louisiana and West Florida.[6]

Carondelet expressed his overall view of Indian policy: "The sustaining of our allied tribes in the possession of their lands is, then, an indispensable object both for the conservation of Louisiana under the power of Spain, and to prevent the Americans from securing the navigation of the Mississippi."[7] The major Indian tribes, with the notable exception of the Cherokees, signed alliances with the Spanish officials at Pensacola and Mobile in 1784. Spain promised to help the Indians oppose American encroachment and to provide annual presents for the tribes, including arms and ammunition.[8]

The United States sought to nullify the Spanish alliances by negotiating their own treaties with the Indians, such as the Treaty of Hopewell (1785 and 1786) with the Chickasaws and the Treaty of New York with the Creeks in 1790. Such apparent duplicity on the part of the Indians angered Carondelet, but Gayoso calmed him when he wrote, "I have always operated under the assumption that the Creeks or Tallapoosas, Choctaws, and Chickasaws are free and independent nations; although they are under His Majesty's protection, we cannot forcibly prevent them from signing a treaty with the United States."[9]

Carondelet believed in tit for tat, however, and he invited a Great Medal Cherokee chief, Bloody Fellow, to visit New Orleans. The Cherokees had not been included in the 1784 alliances because their lands lay within the boundaries of the

United States, but Carondelet sought to include that important tribe in a new alliance. The Cherokees were upset by the loss of good land to the United States by the terms of the Holston Treaty (1791), and Carondelet slyly suggested that he would intercede on the Indians' behalf and try to recover their lands. John McDonald was appointed Spanish agent to the tribe, and plans were developed for building forts on the upper Tombigbee River and at Muscle Shoals on the Tennessee River. The Spanish governor overplayed his good samaritan role, however, and the Chickamauga division of the Cherokees used fifteen horseloads of Spanish ammunition to attack the American settlers of the Cumberland region.[10]

Gayoso pursued a more rational, amicable policy toward the American frontiersmen, and he was one of the few provincial governors to press for joint Spanish-American cooperation regarding the southern Indians.[11] He instructed his agents among the Chickasaws and Choctaws not to denigrate the United States, but to point out the difference between official American policy and the aggressive actions of individual frontiersmen.[12] In an unusual statement to the pro-American Chickasaw chief, Piomingo, Gayoso wrote, "If I am anything else than a Spaniard, I am an American as I have married one."[13]

Theodore Roosevelt exaggerated Carondelet's aggressive policy toward the southern Indians when he quoted from the Spanish governor's statement that, with a few thousand dollars, he could always "rouse the southern tribes to harry the settlers, while at the same time covering his deeds so effectually that the Americans could not point to any specific act of which to complain."[14] In actual practice, however, Gayoso was usually able to soften the warlike stance of Carondelet. He amended the 1793 confederation proposal by deleting the threats against the United States, and in 1794 he wrote directly to the home government to oppose Carondelet's threat to incite the Chickasaws against the American Fort Massac.[15]

During the 1790s, Spanish policy toward the Indians was eclectic, that is, characterized by a variety of techniques learned through trial and error and modified by changing circumstances. Features generally employed were alliance with the southern Indians; appointment of well-paid, capable Indian commissioners and interpreters; supplying the Indians with good quality trade goods at a fair price plus annual presents; granting of medals to notable chiefs; and opposition to land encroachment by the American settlers, to removal of the Indians, and to antisocial behavior by the Indians against the whites and against each other.

The idea of confederation was facilitated by a type of alliance already existing among the Creeks, Choctaws, Chickasaws, and Cherokees, under the ostensible leadership of "King" Tascahetuca of the Chickasaws, who was generally regarded as the "elder brother of all the Indian nations." William Augustus Bowles, a powerful leader of the Lower Creeks, and Gov. gen. Esteban Miró shared a common dream of a vast defensive confederation of all the Indians to prevent American seizure of their land.[16] On 28 October 1793, Spain signed the important Treaty of Nogales at the Walnut Hills, which bound the Creeks, Tallapoosas, Alibamons, Cherokees, Chickasaws, and Choctaws in an alliance of "friendship and guarantee" with Spain. By the terms of article 4, the signatory powers agreed not to take any important action without mutual consultation. Spain agreed to distribute annual presents to the various tribes.[17]

An important feature of the Treaty of Nogales was the appointment of skilled Spanish commissioners and interpreters who would reside among the Indians and work to nullify the influence of the United States. To fill the vacuum created by the death of Creek leader Alexander McGillivray, who had favored Spanish aid, Capt. Pedro Olivier was named in 1793 to cooperate with McGillivray's partner, Gen. Louis Milfort.[18] The opposition of the Creeks to American influence reached a peak when they almost killed James Seagrove, an American agent sent to negotiate with them at Tuckaubatchee later in the year.[19]

Other outstanding Spanish agents and interpreters included Capt. Juan de la Villebeuvre, Simon Favre, and Turner Brashears, who labored among the Choctaws. Benjamin Fooy won the support of an important faction of Chickasaws. Juan

Bernardo Dubroca and Thomas Price interpreted Spanish policy to the Indians of the Mobile District.[20]

Spanish officials insisted that these agents promise nothing to the Indians that they could not fulfill. Written trade schedules insured that the Indians would get proper value for their pelts. The commissioners tried to learn the Indian languages, and some even married Indian women, thus cementing the alliance. The key to satisfying the Indians was to provide them with needed goods at equitable prices. "Any nation that does not furnish them the opportunity to exchange these for what they need," wrote Governor Zéspedes, "cannot hold their attachment, and the Power that provides these for them with most abundance and convenience," he concluded, "will always be the one preferred."[21]

Gayoso expressed a similar view: "The means by which we may gain the Indians' confidence and keep them off the warpath," he wrote, "is to make sure they never lack suitable goods at favorable prices and of a quality to which they are accustomed."[22] Alexander McGillivray also agreed on this vital point when he wrote that "Indians will attach themselves to & Serve them best who Supply their Necessities."[23]

In 1795 Gayoso discovered that the Indians were displeased with some of the goods which Spain had given them. The shirts were too long and the sleeves uncomfortable. Indian women preferred the "mini-skirts" to the "maxi-skirts" which Spain had sent. The Chickasaws admired black silk handkerchiefs. They rejected the Spanish flags which bore the Burgundy Cross in favor of the banners they usually saw flying near Spanish forts, flags which featured the crimson-and-gold lion and castle. Tafia—that fiery, raw rum—had been adulterated with pepper, a fact which angered the Indians and persuaded Gayoso that care should be exercised in the future. It was better to send fewer goods of a higher quality, he argued, than numerous items of an inferior type, for the Indians tended to poke fun at the presents they did not like.[24]

The French and English had customarily given the Indians annual presents, and the Spaniards followed suit. Louisiana's first two Spanish governors, Antonio de Ulloa and Alexander

O'Reilly, met with various tribes and agreed to provide them with annual presents.[25] The cost of such a program soared from only four thousand dollars in 1769 to over fifty-five thousand dollars in 1794, when expenditures for Indian affairs amounted to 10 percent of the total budget for Louisiana and West Florida.[26]

To supply the Indians, Spain made use of non-Spanish firms such as that of Gilbert Antoine de Saint Maxent.[27] After the American Revolution two firms vied for the franchise to supply the Indians. James Mather almost went bankrupt trying to pay the 6 percent import duties and dropped from the competition. William Panton, the canny Scot who had formed the firm of Panton, Leslie and Company gained a considerable fortune supplying the Indians, particularly after his 1790 agreement with Spain exempted him from import duties. By the close of the century he had trading posts from Saint Augustine to the Chickasaw Bluffs and virtually monopolized the Indian trade.[28]

Spanish officials did not intend for Panton to remain in charge, however, and Zéspedes urged the creation of a Spanish firm which would replace the British influence among the southern Indians.[29] Panton's operations continued, however, and his firm completely dominated the trade with the Creeks.[30]

William Augustus Bowles, a native of Maryland who had given himself the title of director general of the state of Muskogee, suggested that Spain open all Florida ports to the nations of the world on a free trade basis.[31] As if to hammer home his point, Bowles led a band of Lower Creeks against Panton's store at Fort San Marcos de Apalache the following year.[32] Carondelet promptly sent a naval expedition under José de Evia, who was captain of the port of New Orleans. Bowles was captured and sent to Morro Castle in Havana and thence to the Philippines. He escaped and returned to plague the Spaniards once more in 1799,[33] but jealous Creek Indians took advantage of the Spanish price on Bowles's head to capture the leader and turn him over to Spanish officials.[34]

One of the major differences between Spanish and American Indian policy was the manner in which Indian lands were obtained. Because Spain did not require lands for farming, when Spanish officials obtained land cessions from the Creeks, Choctaws, or Chickasaws, it was for the purpose of building forts to protect the Indians against American frontiersmen and to supply the Indians with trading goods. Three specific land cessions illustrate this technique. By the 1792 Treaty of Natchez, the Choctaws exchanged a few acres at the Walnut Hills where the Yazoo and Mississippi met for about two thousand dollars in goods plus five hundred dollars "banquet expenses." Gayoso built Fort Nogales on the site of Vicksburg, where Spain could dominate the navigation of the Mississippi, protect the Indians, and oppose the plans of the South Carolina Yazoo Company to settle those traditional hunting lands of the Choctaws.[35]

In 1793 Captain de la Villebeuvre persuaded the Choctaws to sign the Treaty of Boukfouka, by which the thirty acres of land located on the site of the abandoned French Fort Tombecbé, were ceded to Spain. The Spaniards built Fort Confederation on this strategic site to facilitate communication with the Cherokees and to check American expansion. The cost was a mere one thousand dollars.[36]

Another strategic location was the Chickasaw Bluffs, located on the Mississippi River at the present-day location of Memphis. Spain and the United States vied for control of this site, which was a favorite of the Chickasaws. Gayoso led an expedition to the bluffs in 1795, which resulted in the construction of Fort San Fernando de las Barrancas.[37] Despite the opposition from the disappointed Americans and a pro-American faction of the Chickasaws, Spanish Indian policy triumphed on 20 June 1795, when a pro-Spanish faction signed the Chickasaw Bluffs Cession and Spain provided the Chickasaws with a trading post of the Panton, Leslie and Company. Until March 1797, when the post was evacuated in keeping with the Treaty of San Lorenzo, Fort San Fernando dominated the Mississippi and controlled navigation. Once again, Spanish policy had checked American plans for expansion.[38]

A popular feature of Indian policy was the custom of granting medals to prominent Indian chiefs. Spain classified the male Indian adults as to Great Medal, Little Medal, Captains or Notable Warriors, and Warriors.[39] The United States also followed this practice by granting medals with the likeness of George Washington and such legends as "Friendship, Peace and Trade Without End."[40]

Spain also experimented with a removal policy in the 1790s. Unlike the American removal policy of the nineteenth century, Spain did not force the Indians from their homes, nor were the Indian lands a factor. An increase in white settlement and the clearing of protective forests virtually destroyed the Indian hunting grounds, and several years of drought resulting in the loss of livestock and farm produce caused severe privation in the Indian villages. Rather than see the United States supply the Indians with needed provisions, which would result in a corresponding increase in American power and prestige, and unable to supply the Indians with foods which were scarce enough in lower Louisiana, Carondelet suggested to the Caddo and other tribes west of the Mississippi that they allow the Chickasaws to hunt in Arkansas and the Choctaws to hunt in northwestern Louisiana.

The Choctaws usually spent about ten months of the year on these hunts before returning to their homes east of the Mississippi River. Unfortunately, they were not very appreciative guests. They ravaged white and Indian settlements alike, stealing what they wanted, and even killing an innocent family of the Adaes tribe in East Texas. Spanish officials reluctantly abandoned the voluntary removal plan and attempted to restore peace in Louisiana.[41] Accustomed to their raids on the weaker Caddo Nation, however, the Choctaws still continued their westward trek as late as 1798.[42] Only the continuing feud between the Caddo and Osage nations prevented a unified front against the troublesome Choctaws.[43] By 1809 some twelve hundred Choctaws were gathered along the Sabine and Neches rivers, having emigrated from the area of Rapides on the Red River with permission from the governor of Texas.[44]

Spanish officials did not usually meddle in the internal disturbances of the Indians,[45] but they definitely opposed any war

A detail from the painting *A "Diploma" for the Great Medal Chief Opaye-de-mingo,* Issued by the Baron de Carondelet at New Orleans, March 10, 1796. See note 39.

between one tribe and another. When the Tallapoosas went to war against the Chickasaws in 1793 and again in 1795, Carondelet and Gayoso brought pressure on these allies and pointed out that the Treaty of Nogales forbade such activities. The Cumberland settlers, led by Col. James Robertson, took advantage of the Creek-Chickasaw quarrel to improve the American position, and Spain quickly moved to prevent the United States from building forts at Muscle Shoals and the Chickasaw Bluffs.[46]

Frontier commandants tried to maintain Spanish influence among the Indians and to prevent such incidents as occurred in one Chickasaw village when a disgruntled chief, William Glover, tore the Spanish flag into shreds and trod it into the ground. Apparently Glover had been cheated at the Panton store and took his revenge on the Spanish colors.[47]

Renegade bands of Indians continued to raid outlying settlements because they made no distinction regarding the nationality of the frontiersmen. Although the Americans who settled in Spanish Natchez and the Mobile District took an oath of loyalty and became vassals of the Spanish crown, the Indians still looked upon them as Americans, and they vividly recalled how their lands had been taken. Tallapoosas and Choctaws threatened to massacre settlers in the Natchez District.[48] Alibamons from the Mobile District threatened to destroy the settlements along the lower Tombigbee and Tensaw rivers above Mobile, and Governor Miró ordered Fort San Esteban de Tombecbé built in 1789 to protect the settlers.[49] Along the Red, Black, and Ouachita rivers of Louisiana, Indians tried to plunder boats which carried trade goods to and from New Orleans.[50]

White criminals who fled from justice usually found the Indians to be hospitable. Using their villages as bases from which to rob the outlying settlers, these "vagabundos," as the Spaniards called them, even persuaded the eager young braves to accompany them on their raids.[51]

In general, however, Spanish officials were far more successful in controlling the Indians who lived under their jurisdiction than were their American counterparts. Joseph Piernas wrote in 1799 that the Indians of southwestern Louisiana were peaceable and civilized. None had committed any hostile act since Spain had taken Louisiana, he claimed.[52]

Although Spain considered the possible use of Indians as mercenaries to fight against the Americans, the cost was prohibitive. Carondelet wrote that it would cost fifty thousand dollars annually to train and maintain fifteen thousand braves in peacetime and three times that amount during a war.[53]

As a result of the Treaty of San Lorenzo or Pinckney's Treaty of 1795, all the careful, diplomatic work by Spanish officials in Louisiana and West Florida, which had succeeded for a decade in controlling the Indians, was undone. The United States gained the right to navigate the Mississippi River and won control over the Yazoo Strip north of the thirty-first parallel. When Andrew Ellicott arrived in Natchez in February 1797 to begin work on the southern boundary line, he encountered stiff resistance from the Choctaws.[54] Ellicott erroneously concluded that Spain had incited the Indians.

Actually, the opposite was true. Carondelet tried to pacify the Indians by ordering the destruction of Forts San Fernando de las Barrancas and Confederation in March 1797. This would prevent the Americans from using those forts against the Indians, he explained.[55] Gayoso assured the Choctaws and Creeks that the mere fact of drawing a boundary line would not endanger the Indian lands.[56] Gov. Vicente Folch y Juan at Pensacola warned the Tallapoosa not to carry out their threat to "burn powder" against the boundary commissions or Spain would join forces with the Americans to annihilate the tribe. The Indians were not impressed, however, and at Tuckabatchee in the summer of 1798 they voted to oppose the Americans anyway.[57]

The most serious disturbance encountered by the boundary commission took place near the confluence of the Flint, Chattahoochee, and Apalachicola rivers during 1799, where Seminoles and Lower Creeks stole horses and equipment and so harried the commissioners that they sailed around Florida and concluded their boundary operations from the Saint Mary's River.[58]

Spanish officials reinforced the frontier forts at Natchez Nogales, and Arkansas to prevent hostilities from the Indians, but the United States misinterpreted this move as a ploy to delay the evacuation of posts north of the thirty-first parallel.[59] At Fort Stoddart, just north of the boundary line in Alabama, Capt. Bartholomew Schaumburgh reported that the Creeks had grown so insolent that he wished "to have had it in my power to send them to hell." By a close vote the Alibamons had barely defeated a proposal to attack the Americans at Fort Stoddart, and the entire frontier was on the alert.[60]

Spanish success in dealing with the Indians owed much to the individual efforts of agents, interpreters, and government officials, many of whom learned the various languages, dialects, customs, and nuances of expression. Fooy and de la Ville- beuvre, for example, accomplished much in their conferences with the Chickasaws and Choctaws. Governor Gayoso was one of the most talented diplomats with whom the Indians dealt in the 1790s. He insisted on protecting Indian rights, even if it meant arresting one of his own sheriffs and sending him out of the district because of his inflammatory statements to the Indian chiefs.[61] When a Spanish soldier shot and wounded the son of a prominent Choctaw chief in 1791, the zealous governor filed charges against the aggressor and provided health care in the Natchez Royal Hospital for the injured youth.[62] He once gave a valuable sabre and its silver-mounted scabbard to a Choctaw chief who had expressed admiration of the weapon.[63]

Above all, Spanish officers who kept their sense of humor and shared it with the Indians won their admiration and support. The Choctaws gave Gayoso a special name, Chacti- mataha, which he took to mean "king of the Choctaws" in his report of the 1793 Nogales Conference.[64] This personal touch may have been the most important factor of all in the success of Spanish policy toward the southern Indians during the 1790s.

NOTES

1. R. S. Cotterill, "Federal Indian Management in the South, 1789–1825," *Mississippi Valley Historical Review* 20 (1933): 333.

2. Zéspedes to Antonio Valdés y Bazán (Minister of the Indies), no. 7, St. Augustine, 24 March 1788, Archivo General de Indias (Sevilla), Papeles procedentes de la Isla de Cuba (hereafter cited as AGI, PC), legajo 2359.

3. O'Neill to Bernardo de Gálvez, Pensacola, 8 July 1785, AGI, PC, leg. 37, and translated in "Papers from the Spanish Archives Relating to Tennessee and the Old Southwest, 1783–1800," ed. and trans. Duvon C. and Roberta Corbitt, *Publications of the East Tennessee Historical Society*, no. 9 (1937), p. 123.

4. Jane M. Berry, "Indian Policy of Spain in the Southwest, 1783–1795," *Mississippi Valley Historical Review* 3 (1917): 465–466.

5. Jack D. L. Holmes, *Gayoso: The Life of a Spanish Governor in the Mississippi Valley, 1789–1799* (Baton Rouge: Louisiana State University Press for the Louisiana Historical Association, 1965), pp. 3–33, 136–161.

6. Jack D. L. Holmes, ed., *Documentos inéditos para la historia de la Luisiana, 1792–1810* (Madrid: Ediciones José Porrúa Turanzas, 1963), pp. 144–145.

7. Carondelet to Luis de las Casas, no. 135, confidential, New Orleans, 13 June 1795, AGI, PC, leg. 1447. This letter is translated in *The Spanish Regime in Missouri*, ed. Louis Houck, 2 vols. (Chicago: R. R. Donnelley and Sons, 1909), 2: 111–113.

8. Jack D. L. Holmes, "Spanish Treaties with West Florida Indians, 1784–1802," *Florida Historical Quarterly* 48 (1969): 140–154.

9. Gayoso to Duque de Alcudia (Manuel de Godoy, Minister of State), no. 2, Natchez, 14 May 1793, AGI, PC, leg. 177; Holmes, *Gayoso*, p. 157.

10. A. P. Whitaker, "Spain and the Cherokee Indians, 1783–98," *North Carolina Historical Review* 4 (1927): 252–269.

11. Berry, "Indian Policy of Spain," p. 474; Holmes, *Gayoso*, pp. 160–161.

12. Berry, "Indian Policy of Spain," p. 474.

13. Gayoso to Piomingo, Fort Ferdinand of the Bluffs, 23 June 1795, AGI, PC, leg. 211; Holmes, *Gayoso*, p. 124.

14. Theodore Roosevelt, *Winning of the West*, 4 vols. (New York: G. P. Putnam's Sons, 1895–1896), 3: 135–136.

15. Holmes, *Gayoso*, p. 159; Berry, "Indian Policy of Spain," p. 476.

16. Mary A. M. O'Callaghan, "The Indian Policy of Carondelet in Spanish Louisiana, 1792–1797" (Ph.D. diss., University of California, Berkeley, 1942), pp. 47–48; Holmes, *Gayoso*, pp. 150–151.

17. Holmes, *Gayoso*, pp. 150–154; S.V. "Nogales, Treaty of"; Holmes, "Treaties with West Florida Indians," pp. 148–149.

18. Carondelet to Alcudia, no. 1, confidential, New Orleans, 28 February 1793, and no. 2, confidential, New Orleans, 9 March 1793, Archivo Histórico Nacional (Madrid), Sección de Estado (hereafter cited as AHN, EST.), leg. 3898; Gen. Louis Milfort, *Mémoire ou coup-d'Oeil Rapide sur mes différens voyages et mon séjour dans la nation Crëek*, trans. and ed. from the

1802 Paris edition by Ben C. McCary (Kennesaw, Ga.: Printed for the translator, 1959).

19. Daniel M. Smith, "James Seagrove and the Mission to Tuckaubatchee, 1793," *Georgia Historical Quarterly* 44 (1960): 41–55.

20. Holmes, *Gayoso*, pp. 153–154; idem., "Notes on the Spanish Fort San Esteban de Tombecbé," *Alabama Review* 18 (1965): 285.

21. Zéspedes to Valdés, no. 7, Saint Augustine, 24 March 1788, AGI, PC, leg. 2359. This letter also appears in "Papers from the Spanish Archives," ed. and trans. Duvon C. and Roberta Corbitt, *Publications of the East Tennessee Historical Society*, no. 14 (1942), pp. 86–94.

22. Gayoso to Conde de Floridablanca (Minister of State), New Orleans, 8 May 1789, AHN, EST., leg. 3902; Holmes, *Gayoso*, p. 141.

23. Alexander McGillivray to Arturo O'Neill, Little Tallassie, 1 January 1784, John Walton Caughey, *McGillivray of the Creeks* (Norman: University of Oklahoma Press, 1938), p. 65.

24. Gayoso to Carondelet, no. 9, New Madrid, 22 September 1795, AGI, PC, leg. 34.

25. Jack D. L. Holmes, *A Guide to Spanish Louisiana, 1762–1806* (New Orleans: Louisiana Collection Series, 1970), p. 4.

26. Holmes, "Treaties with West Florida Indians," p. 149; idem., *Gayoso*, p. 154.

27. Caroline Maude Burson, *The Stewardship of Don Esteban Miró, 1782–1792* (New Orleans: American Printing, 1940), pp. 49–51.

28. Petition of Santiago Mather, New Orleans, 24 July 1784, AGI, PC, leg. 184–A; Holmes, *Gayoso*, p. 141.

29. Zéspedes to Valdés, no. 7, 24 March 1788.

30. Benjamin Hawkins, the American commissioner to the Creeks, wrote in 1797, "Mr. William Panton has engrossed the greatest part of the trade of this nation, his establishment is at Pensacola; he supplies not only the white traders, but he has set up a number of Indian factors. They are both behind-hand with him, and the Indians are indebted to them to a considerable amount." Hawkins to Secretary of War [James McHenry], no. 2, Coweta, 6 January 1797, *Letters of Benjamin Hawkins, 1796–1806*, vol. 9, *Collections of the Georgia Historical Society* (Savannah, 1916), 57. See also, Holmes, *Gayoso*, p. 141. In 1798 the American commissioner to the Choctaws recommended the continued use of Panton's firm to calm Indian outcries against the United States regarding the boundary line. Samuel Mitchell to William Panton, John Pitchlynn's in the Choctaw Nation, 13 March 1798, Forbes Collection, Mobile Public Library.

31. Jack D. L. Holmes and J. Leitch Wright, Jr., trans. and eds., "Luis Bertucat and William Augustus Bowles: West Florida Adversaries in 1791," *Florida Historical Quarterly* 44 (1970): 49–62; J. Leitch Wright, Jr., *William Augustus Bowles: Director General of the Creek Nation* (Athens: University of Georgia Press, 1967).

32. Lawrence Kinnaird, "The Significance of William Augustus Bowles' Seizure of Panton's Apalachee Store in 1792," *Florida Historical Quarterly* 9 (1931): 156–192.

33. Jack D. L. Holmes, ed., *José de Evia y sus reconocimientos del Golfo de México, 1783–1796* (Madrid: Ediciones José Porrúa Turanzas, 1968), pp. 193–230.

34. Wright, *Bowles*, pp. 77–174.

35. Holmes, *Gayoso*, pp. 145–150; Holmes, "Treaties with West Florida Indians," pp. 151–152.

36. Ibid., p. 152.

37. Ibid., pp. 152–153; Jack D. L. Holmes, "Spanish-American Rivalry over the Chickasaw Bluffs, 1780–1795," *Publications of the East Tennessee Historical Society*, no. 34 (1962) , pp. 26–57.

38. Jack D. L. Holmes, "The Ebb-Tide of Spanish Military Power on the Mississippi: Fort San Fernando de las Barrancas, 1795–1798," *Publications of the East Tennessee Historical Society*, no. 36 (1964) , pp. 23–44.

39. A *"Diploma" for the Great Medal Chief Opaye-de-mingo, Issued by the Baron de Carondelet at New Orleans, March 10, 1796*, a painting, is in AGI, Section of Planos, Mexico, no. 549. The entire diploma has been published in "The Choctaws in 1795," ed. Jack D. L. Holmes, *Alabama Historical Quartery* 30 (1968) : 5. A modification by the artist Manuel Bueno appears in Holmes, "Die Eingliederung Floridas in die Vereinigten Staaten von Amerika," *Die Zinnfigur* (Hanover, Germany) , Heft 12/15, 12.1968, 252. For the Choctaw hierarchy of chiefs, see *Alabama Historical Quarterly* 30 (1968) : 33–49.

40. Illustrations of three American medals are printed in Miguel Gómez del Campillo, comp., *Relaciones diplomáticas entre España y los Estados Unidos según los documentos del Archivo Histórico Nacional*, 2 vols. (Madrid: Consejo Superior de Investigaciones Científicas, Instituto Gonzalo Fernández de Oviedo, 1944, 1946) , 1: opposite 270.

41. Mary A. M. O'Callaghan, "An Indian Removal Policy in Spanish Louisiana," *Greater America, Essays in Honor of Herbert Eugene Bolton* (Berkeley: University of California Press, 1945) , pp. 281–294. Carondelet threatened the Choctaws with loss of their annual presents if they refused to end their raids on the Caddo Nation. Carondelet to Pedro Olivier, New Orleans, 19 April 1797, AGI, PC, leg. 2365.

42. Stephen Minor to Gayoso, Camp, Thompson's Creek, 24 October 1798, AGI, PC, leg. 215–A; Holmes, ed., *Documentos de la Luisiana*, p. 346; Holmes, *Gayoso*, pp. 155–156.

43. Carlos de Grand-Pré to Carondelet, nos. 23 and 37, Avoyelles, 27 September and 21 November 1796, AGI, PC, leg. 34. On the history of the Caddos, see William B. Glover, "A History of the Caddo Indians," *Louisiana Historical Quarterly* 18 (1935) : 872–946.

44. Walter Prescott Webb, ed., *The Handbook of Texas*, 2 vols. (Austin: Texas State Historical Association, 1952) , 1: 344.

45. For example, in 1791 a dispute between a drunk Choctaw and an inebriated Cherokee was settled by the Indians themselves. Holmes, *Gayoso*, p. 157.

46. Knoxville *Gazette*, 2 October 1795; Albert V. Goodpasture, "Indian Wars and Warriors of the Old Southwest, 1730–1807," *Tennessee Historical Magazine* 4 (1918) : 285–289; Holmes, *Gayoso*, p. 155.

47. Jack D. L. Holmes, "Three Early Memphis Commandants: Beauregard, DeVille DeGoutin, and Folch," *Papers of the West Tennessee Historical Society* 18 (1964) : 31.

48. Gayoso to Carondelet, no. 203, Natchez, 27 November 1792, AGI, PC, leg. 41; Holmes, *Gayoso*, p. 144.

49. Holmes, "Notes on Fort San Esteban de Tombecbé," p. 282.

50. Gayoso to Carondelet, no. 209, Natchez, 6 December 1792, AGI, PC, leg. 41.

51. Francisco Bouligny to Miró, Fort Panmure de Natchez, 22 August 1785, *Spain in the Mississippi Valley, 1765–1794*, ed. Lawrence Kinnaird, vols. 2–4, *American Historical Association Annual Report for 1945*, 3 pts. (Washington: Government Printing Office, 1946–1949), pt. 2, p. 137.

52. Petition of Piernas, Bayou aux Boeuf, 4 December 1799, copy enclosed in Joseph Vidal to Marqués de Casa-Calvo, no. 74, Natchez, 11 March 1800, Louisiana Collection, Bancroft Library (Berkeley), box 5, folder 542. It has been edited by Jack D. L. Holmes, "The Calcasieu Promoter: Joseph Piernas and his 1799 Proposal," *Louisiana History* 9 (1968): 163–167.

53. Holmes, *Gayoso*, p. 142.

54. Ibid., pp. 184, 194.

55. Carondelet to Gayoso, New Orleans, 30 December 1796, AGI, PC, leg. 23; Holmes, "Ebb-Tide of Spanish Military Power," pp. 38–41.

56. Gayoso to Minor, New Orleans, 6 June 1798, copy enclosed in Gayoso to Príncipe de la Paz (Manuel de Godoy), no. 22, New Orleans, 6 June 1798, AHN, EST., leg. 3900; Gayoso to Pedro Olivier, New Orleans, 30 January 1798, AGI, PC, leg. 2354.

57. Folch to Gayoso, no. 169, Pensacola, 20 August 1798, copy enclosed in Gayoso to Manuel de Godoy, no. 29, confidential, New Orleans, 26 September 1798, ibid.; Holmes, *Gayoso*, p. 235.

58. Ibid., pp. 235–236; Ellicott to Benjamin Hawkins, Pensacola Bay, 3 June 1799, Louisiana Collection, Bancroft Library, box 5; Jack D. L. Holmes, "The Southern Boundary Commission, the Chattahoochee, and the Seminoles, 1799," *Florida Historical Quarterly* 44 (1966): 312–341.

59. Holmes, *Gayoso*, p. 185.

60. Jack D. L. Holmes, ed., "Fort Stoddart in 1799: Seven Letters of Captain Bartholomew Schaumburgh," *Alabama Historical Quarterly* 26 (1964): 236, 249–250.

61. Gayoso to Carondelet, no. 11, Natchez, 24 March 1792, AGI, PC, leg. 41.

62. Gayoso to Miró, nos. 101, 151, Natchez, 14 May and 22 July 1791, AGI, PC, leg. 41.

63. Juan de la Villebeuvre to Carondelet, Boukfouka, 25 January 1793, AGI, PC, leg. 147–A.

64. Holmes, *Gayoso*, pp. 159–160.

SOURCES CITED

Berry, Jane M. "Indian Policy of Spain in the Southwest, 1783–1795." *Mississippi Valley Historical Review* 3 (March 1917): 462–477.

Burson, Caroline Maude. *The Stewardship of Don Esteban Miró, 1782–1792*. New Orleans: American Printing, 1940.

Caughey, John Walton. *McGillivray of the Creeks*. Norman: University of Oklahoma Press, 1938.

Corbitt, Duvon C., and Corbitt, Roberta, ed. and trans.. "Papers from the Spanish Archives Relating to Tennessee and the Old Southwest, 1783–

1800." *Publications of the East Tennessee Historical Society*, no. 9 (1937), pp. 111–142; no. 14 (1942), pp. 86–101.

Cotterill, R. S. "Federal Indian Management in the South, 1789–1825." *Mississippi Valley Historical Review* 20 (December 1933): 333–352.

Glover, William B. "A History of the Caddo Indians." *Louisiana Historical Quarterly* 18 (October 1935): 872–946.

Gómez del Campillo, Miguel. *Relaciones diplomáticas entre España y los Estados Unidos según los documentos del Archivo Histórico Nacional.* 2 vols. Madrid: Consejo Superior de Investigaciones Científicas Instituto Gonzalo Fernández de Oviedo, 1944, 1946.

Goodpasture, Albert V. "Indian Wars and Warriors of the Old Southwest, 1730–1807." *Tennessee Historical Magazine* 4 (1918): 3–49, 106–145, 161–210, 252–289.

Hawkins, Benjamin. *Letters of Benjamin Hawkins, 1796–1806. Collections of the Georgia Historical Society*, vol. 9. Savannah: Georgia Historical Society, 1916.

Holmes, Jack D. L. "The Choctaws in 1795." *Alabama Historical Quarterly* 30 (Spring 1968): 5, 33–49.

———. *Documentos inéditos para la historia de la Luisiana, 1792–1810. Colección Chimalistac*, vol. 15. Madrid: Ediciones José Porrúa Turanzas, 1963.

———. "The Ebb-Tide of Spanish Military Power on the Mississippi: Fort San Fernando de las Barrancas, 1795–1798." *Publications of the East Tennessee Historical Society*, no. 36 (1964), pp. 23–44.

———. "Fort Stoddart in 1799: Seven Letters of Captain Bartholomew Schaumburgh." *Alabama Historical Quarterly* 26 (fall-winter 1964): 231–252.

———. *Gayoso: The Life of a Spanish Governor in the Mississippi Valley, 1789–1799.* Baton Rouge: Louisiana State University Press for the Louisiana Historical Association, 1965.

———. *A Guide to Spanish Louisiana, 1762–1806. Louisiana Collection Series*, vol. 2. New Orleans: Louisiana Collection Series, 1970.

———. *José de Evia y sus reconocimientos del Golfo de México, 1783–1796. Colección Chimalistac*, vol. 26. Madrid: Ediciones José Porrúa Turanzas, 1968.

———. "Notes on the Spanish Fort San Esteban de Tombecbé." *Alabama Review* 18 (October 1965): 281–290.

———. "The Southern Boundary Commission, the Chattahoochee River, and the Florida Seminoles, 1799." *Florida Historical Quarterly* 44 (April 1966) 312–341.

———. "Spanish-American Rivalry over the Chickasaw Bluffs, 1780–1795." *Publications of the East Tennessee Historical Society*, no. 34 (1962), pp. 26–57.

———. "Spanish Treaties with West Florida Indians, 1784–1802." *Florida Historical Quarterly* 48 (October 1969): 140–154.

———. "Three Early Memphis Commandants: Beauregard, DeVille De-Goutin, and Folch." *Papers of the West Tennessee Historical Society* 18 (1964): 5–38.

———, and Wright, J. Leitch, trans. and eds. "Luis Bertucat and William Augustus Bowles: West Florida Adversaries in 1791." *Florida Historical Quarterly* 49 (July 1970): 49–62.

Houck, Louis, ed. *The Spanish Regime in Missouri.* 2 vols. Chicago: R. R. Donnelley and Sons, 1909.

Kinnaird, Lawrence. "The Significance of William Augustus Bowles' Seizure of Panton's Apalachee Store in 1792." *Florida Historical Society Quarterly* 9 (1931): 156–192.

———. *Spain in the Mississippi Valley, 1765–1794.* 3 vols. *American Historical Association Annual Report for 1945.* Washington: Government Printing Office, 1946–1949.

Milfort, Gen. Louis. *Mémoire ou coup-d'Oeil Rapide sur mes différens voyages et mon séjour dans la nation Crëek.* Translated by Ben C. McCary. Kennesaw, Ga.: Printed for the translator, 1959.

O'Callaghan, Mary A. M. "The Indian Policy of Carondelet in Spanish Louisiana, 1792–1797." Ph.D. dissertation, University of California, 1942.

———. "An Indian Removal Policy in Spanish Louisiana." *Greater America* (Berkeley: University of California Press, 1945), pp. 281–294.

Roosevelt, Theodore. *The Winning of the West.* 4 vols. New York: G. P. Putnam's Sons, 1894–1896.

Smith, Daniel M. "James Seagrove and the Mission to Tuckaubatchee, 1793." *Georgia Historical Quarterly* 44 (March 1960): 41–55.

Webb, Walter Prescott. *The Handbook of Texas.* 2 vols. Austin: Texas State Historical Association, 1952.

Whitaker, Arthur P. "Spain and the Cherokee Indians, 1783–1798." *North Carolina Historical Review* 4 (July 1927): 252–269.

Wright, J. Leitch, Jr. *William Augustus Bowles: Director General of the Creek Nation.* Athens: University of Georgia Press, 1967.

Myths and Realities in Indian Westward Removal: The Choctaw Example

Arthur H. DeRosier, Jr.

Though the American Indian has been a central figure in North American history longer than any other people, less is known about him than Anglo-Americans, black Americans, Jewish Americans, and probably any other group that has contributed to the evolution of this nation's history. Many have suggested that historical neglect is the main reason we know little about Indians; it seems to me, though, that such an answer might be seriously challenged if it is not carefully qualified. Quantitatively, a great deal has been written on red Americans. If one weighs interest by the pound or by the book, Indians have not been neglected. Countless historians, anthropologists, poets, antiquarians, reformers, novelists, diarists, and others with a pen or a typewriter have tried their hand at projecting the "real" Indian. He has adorned drugstores, book jackets, World War II bombers, movie screens, athletic teams, and coins. Certainly we cannot suggest that he has been the forgotten American. However, if one measures neglect qualitatively, then the Indian has been the victim of almost constant neglect. How many historians have devoted their scholarly careers to red Americans as opposed, let us say, to the American Revolution or the Progressive era? Many of our finest western frontier historians will own up to the fact that they know more about Conestoga wagons, gold mining, and the Lost State of Franklin than they do about Indians. Fortunately, more and more young scholars have been attracted to Indian subjects and our original citizens are starting to emerge as real human beings caught up in the drama of history.

I suspect that all fields of historical interest have their Parson Weems figures who knead, mold, and shape people and events to fit preconceived images, but no field has been so plagued as native American studies. Out of past writings have emerged two equally disastrous myths that have haunted serious students of Indian history from time immemorial—the myth of the murderous red savage and the myth of the noble red creature of the forest. Both of these myths, unfortunately, are still with us and are portrayed daily to our children by well-meaning elementary, secondary, and college teachers who stumble periodically upon the topic. The truth of the matter is that Indians are just like other people: some are good and others bad; some are short and others tall; some are honest and others dishonest; some are geniuses and others not so bright. One need not belabor the point, but surely the time has come when understanding is more desirable than mythology, particularly since the general public is more interested today in the Indian than ever before. Fortunately, the small coterie of good Indian historians are training even better ones; we are starting to receive a steady stream of excellent volumes on Indian subjects. However, popular presses, ever conscious of sales and volume, are still publishing thoughtless, unscholarly works and reprinting past scholarly disasters for a hungry public.

Recently, I began a study of current junior high, senior high, and college American history survey textbooks, to find out what kind of coverage is being given to Indians generally and to Indian removal from eastern states to the West specifically. When the task is completed, I want, then, to compare the findings with popular texts used ten years ago and back through previous decades. I want, also, to question teachers of survey courses to determine whether they present to their students information in addition to that which is included in the textbook. Though the project is hardly underway, I have already noted that a number of misconceptions uncovered by recent research are still portrayed as gospel not only by teachers but also by the textbooks they use. Though there is nothing surprising in this fact, I would like to address myself to some of these misconceptions and generalizations that were uncovered in my research on the Choctaw removal story.[1]

One of the myths that bothers me most concerns the means by which the United States secured Indian lands. Though a number of oversimplified generalities are offered about military acquisition of land east of the Mississippi River, I am more concerned here about lands secured through negotiation. Many writers simply state that the United States government considered Indian tribes as independent nations and negotiated with them as equals when more land was desired by frontiersmen. Such a statement simply will not suffice because, in the first place, Indian tribes were not treated as foreign nations; they were handled by the War Department and not the State Department. If one is to understand eastern removals, it is important to realize that tribes did not simply negotiate at the beck and call of the Washington government and move west after a treaty was signed and ratified.

Actually the negotiation story is a quite complicated one. First, tribal leaders were approached a number of times by Indian agents, War Department representatives, or special commissioners requesting a cession of land. At the same time the government might establish a factory, or store, in the nation and advertise that tribesmen were welcome to frequent these stores, purchase goods on credit, and pay for them at some undetermined later date. From 1795 to 1822 the "factory system" played a central role in encouraging tribes to cede lands to the United States.[2] If the writers of textbooks even mention these factories, and most of them do not, they present them as present-day discount houses where tribesmen were granted the privilege of securing needed commodities at moderate prices. Leland Baldwin in *The Stream of American History* states that they "were government-operated trading posts . . . where the Indians could obtain honest goods at honest prices."[3] What he failed to mention is that the government had sinister reasons for establishing these factories. Pres.

Thomas Jefferson took great pains to encourage Indians to buy all their goods from these stores; to facilitate debt he offered unlimited credit. Then, when Indian debts became so burdensome that they could not possibly be paid, Indian agents were instructed to reveal that the government would magnanimously liquidate the debts by accepting land cessions. Jefferson wrote William Henry Harrison on 27 February 1803, "We shall push our trading houses, and be glad to see the good and influential individuals among them run in debt, because we observe that when these debts get beyond what the individual can pay they become willing to lop them off by a cession of lands."[4] When one realizes what the government attempted to do with these factories, at the same time that they were bombarding tribesmen with requests for Indian lands, the real story begins to emerge. By calling in debts the Choctaws owed to factories in 1803, the United States was able to secure 853,-760 acres of land in the Treaty of Hoe Buckintoopa, in exchange for canceled debts and a modest amount of additional goods.[5]

If the Indian factories played an important role in government efforts to secure Indian lands, so did the constant pressure for negotiation. Not only were the pressures unrelenting but they were also diversified. The whole process represented almost a ritual. Indian leaders and councils were approached with a request for a "modest" amount of land accompanied with promises of generous remunerations. These tactics were used even though acquisition of small pieces of land was not the government's real aim, after the purchase of the Louisiana lands in 1803. Evacuation of all eastern lands for a new home in the West was the real goal,[6] but before 1816 the government hardly even mentioned that fact. Rather, in typical Jefferson fashion, that end was approached in a roundabout way: the United States was to secure eastern tribal homes by acquiring periodic bits and pieces of nations.[7] Hardly a year passed from 1800 until eventual removal in 1830 when the Choctaws were not being harried to cede more land. Each treaty negotiation was accompanied by promises that this cession would be the last one requested, but as soon as the tribes consented, agents appeared again requesting additional cessions. During the first thirty years of the nineteenth century, the Choctaws were approached no less than forty times with requests to negotiate for land cessions. The relentless pressure forced the tribe to acquiesce periodically, even though the leaders knew that frontier appetites would not be appeased until all Indian lands belonged to white planters and farmers. On five occasions before 1830, the Choctaws ceded Mississippi land amounting to a total of more than 13,000,000 acres, but the pressure for the remaining 10,423,130 acres never abated.

Not only do general studies fail to mention the constant pressure and the piecemeal way in which most land was secured, but they fail to describe the various pressures exerted on tribes to negotiate. First, requests for land were usually accompanied by promises that the tribe was at liberty to refuse if it so desired.[8] At about the same time, an Indian factory appeared and soon there were more requests for negotiation accompanied by dire predictions of uncontrolled lawlessness by land-hungry frontiersmen if the requests went unheeded. If the tribesmen held firm and refused to negotiate, new and tougher commissioners, often military heroes such as Andrew Jackson, appeared on the scene with bribery allowances and verbal threats. During the negotiations of 1820 Jackson flatly told the Choctaw leaders that they must accept his terms or "be lost forever. This is the last attempt . . . that will be made to treat on this side of the Mississippi," he warned.[9] By this statement he implied that a failure to cede would be followed by an invasion that would force all tribesmen to remove to Indian Territory. In the meantime government agents were weighing the responses of each individual Indian negotiator trying to find those who were weakening and might be susceptible to a bribe or special considerations. Once the Indian ranks were broken, the tide was turned and United States victory was in sight. What I am suggesting is that the idea that equal nations sat down and honestly discussed the cession of Indian land is a myth that cannot be substantiated.

Another equally indefensible myth often presented as fact is that eastern tribes were removed to permanent new homes in the West there to stay forevermore. More often than not tribes were granted large holdings of land in the West only to lose portions of that land at various times throughout the remainder of the nineteenth century. The Choctaws serve as a good example of this process of western contraction. In the 1820 Treaty of Doak's Stand, the Choctaws ceded 5,169,788 acres of Mississippi land for approximately 13,000,000 acres of land in the southern half of the present state of Oklahoma and southwestern Arkansas Territory.[10] However, the cession was offered not because the negotiators believed the Choctaws should actually settle all that land but because it was the kind of enticement necessary to secure Choctaw acquiescence. Jackson knew the boundaries of Arkansas Territory as established by Congress in March of 1819. As David Baird points out in his excellent article in the *Arkansas Historical Quarterly*, the original Territory of Arkansas encompassed one hundred thousand square miles, including most of present-day Oklahoma.[11] Despite this fact, Jackson hesitated not a moment to cede the Choctaws forty thousand square miles in the southwest quadrant of Arkansas Territory. Incidentally, he also included part of the Spanish Empire farther west in the 13,000,000-acre Choctaw cession.[12]

The importance of this western cession to the Choctaws—and other examples that illustrate the same point—cannot be overemphasized if one is to understand America's eastern removal policy. The simple fact is that the United States had no intention of allowing tribes to be permanently settled on all, if any, lands ceded to them in the West. I say "any" because of evidence such as a letter written by Jefferson to John Breckenridge in 1803. "When we shall be full on this side," the great Virginian wrote, "we may lay off a range of States on the western bank [of the Mississippi River] from the head to the mouth, and so, range after range, advancing compactly as we multiply." The pressing need of the moment, he suggested, was to push the Indians across the Mississippi and open up all eastern lands to settlement. Then, when population caught up with the Indians, they would be removed again and again to the Pacific Coast and beyond.[13] If the United States were following this idea suggested by President Jefferson—and I believe it was—then ceding to the Choctaws the land that belonged to territories and even other countries is perfectly logical because that home was only temporary anyway. Of course, we know today that the Indians were not pushed relentlessly westward; American settlement did not follow that pattern. But how was Jefferson to know that fact in 1803, or how were Calhoun, Jackson, and Monroe to know it in 1820?

The fact that the Choctaws, Cherokees, Miamis, Kickapoos, Creeks, and others did not end up on Alcatraz or Samoa is not really important. What is important is that the Choctaws and other tribes did not end up on all land ceded to them in the West either. The people of Arkansas Territory complained that Indians had been given forty thousand square miles of its land, but in the end all of the land was returned to Arkansas Territory.[14] Also, the Choctaws eventually had to share their land with the Chickasaws.[15] They eventually retained southeastern Oklahoma which was only a portion of their original grant. The periodic loss of western land to other tribes and white settlers is an important fact to consider when one endeavors to understand the reluctance of tribes to sell the remainder of their eastern lands, and when one studies the many problems that accompanied starting over again in the West.

Another misconception that deserves serious reexamination is the often repeated suggestion that military officers and civilian removal agents were inhuman in their treatment of migrating tribesmen during those sad "trails of tears" that followed final removal treaties. To be sure, there were individuals who cared not whether migrating Choctaws arrived in Fort Smith alive or were buried in shallow graves along the way. But such was the exception and not the rule. The story of the Choctaw removals of 1831, 1832, and 1833 are filled with innumerable instances where agents did everything possible to insure that life and property were safeguarded. What was wrong with these removals is that they were badly planned by officials in Washington and elsewhere.[16] After all, the Choctaw removal was one of the government's first experiences with moving thousands of Indians across rivers and strange country. Even when one allows a good deal of latitude for governmental inexperience, however, one is still left with the fact that the removals were plagued by inefficiency, waste, and incredible misinformation. Only about one-third enough money was appropriated for the job.[17] Tents, clothing, wagons, and equipment were sent ahead to Fort Smith to greet the Indians on their arrival, when most of those goods were needed for the trip itself. When the routes were announced, Arkansas citizens doubled and tripled the price of corn, beef, pork, and bread that was to be purchased along the way. Even Mother Nature vented her fury on removing Indians by providing ice and snow storms, constant rains, and muddy quagmires that once were roads. But one cannot blame the removal agents for governmental inefficiency and bad weather. After all, they were simply charged with escorting the tribesmen and not with planning or financing the trek.

The accounts of bravery and compassion by removal agents are numerous. Some purchased goods along the way without authorization or money to do so. Some hired steamboats and charged the expenses to the government. Some selected unauthorized routes when it appeared to them that such a move would save lives and suffering. Lt. L. T. Cross is a good example of a removal agent in action. He commanded a group of nine hundred Choctaws to be moved through Louisiana and Arkansas to Indian Territory during the first Choctaw removal in 1831. When he reached Ecore à Fabre in Arkansas with his removal party intact, Cross received news that another small party of two hundred Indians was lost in northern Louisiana. He called for volunteers from among the male Indians with him and set out after the lost party without instructions to do so. He found them in dire straits in the swamps around Lake Providence and marched them to Monroe, Louisiana. He then chartered the steamboat *Talma* and took the group to join his own nearly starved charges. Cross faced the challenge of transporting these eleven hundred exhausted Choctaws to Indian Territory without any money, food, or even instructions. In this emergency, he took the initiative; without authorization he hired wagons and horses and purchased food on the credit of the United States government. But being in no position to bargain, he was forced to pay exorbitant prices to the local citizens for these goods; each Indian ration, for example, cost him twelve and one-half cents —more than twice the normal price of six cents. Early in February 1832, he and his Indians set out for their objective, Fort Towson, a trip that was to take them 165 miles over treacherous roads.[18] For his efforts Lieutenant Cross and other agents were censured on a dozen counts. Although he and his colleagues had cost the government almost three times the amount allowed for the removal, he had saved lives and showed a humanity we usually deny him and his military colleagues by blaming them for other people's mistakes.

Emphasizing that there were military personnel who did not hate Indians does not mean that we should view frontier soldiers as Indian benefactors. The truth of the matter is that most soldiers did consider Indians inferior beings who were nothing more than stone age relics that had to be handled like any other obstacles to an advancing civilization. But the same can be said for American society in general. Most Americans felt little remorse for the plight of Indians; they surely did not feel that a great culture and a significant historical tradition were being destroyed by greedy interlopers. The military arm of the United States simply mirrored society in general. They left a trail of bloody conquest and death because the civilian population they served demanded that they do so. It is therefore unfair to make them the scapegoats of the tragedy, suggesting that they made a mockery of American law and our innate sense of fair play. That is simply not true. The military did what white America wanted them to do, and they did it in a way that was applauded and appreciated by most citizens. However, once the dirty deed was done and society had an opportunity to reflect on the horror of it all, it became fashionable to cleanse oneself of the stain by blaming the military for excesses, brutality, and a disregard for humane orders. This is a myth that has grown up in the twentieth century; it needs to be exposed before it becomes more deeply ingrained in American history.

The simple truth is that military personnel, like all other members of society, are not all one thing or another. Some liked Indians and felt compassion towards them; others hated Indians and felt that by killing them they were serving the just ends of society; most thought little on the subject and simply carried out the orders handed them by their commanders. However, the military is not the only group society thinks of in black and white terms. Indian agents and missionaries have suffered the same fate. History has portrayed both these groups in the same absolutist terms it has the military. Before leaving the subject of what might be called the black-white myth, a brief look is warranted at specific Indian agents and missionaries who worked with the Choctaws to see if modifications are in order.

A study of the Choctaw Indians before removal offers an excellent opportunity to compare Indian agents. The agent from 1801 until 1821 was John McKee; his successor until removal was William Ward. Owing to the human tendency to accept a stereotype rather than to judge on individual performance, McKee has emerged as an agent who worked incessantly for the destruction of the Mississippi Choctaw Nation. His biographer in the *Dictionary of American Biography* stated that from the end of the Creek War onward "he lent his energies toward the final removal of the Five Civilized tribes to reservations beyond the Mississippi."[19] The statement is simply not supported by the source material available. For twenty years he participated in all United States efforts to secure Choctaw land. Also, as was the case with any Indian agent, he was charged with representing the interests of the government in all matters relating to that tribe. In these endeavors McKee emerges as a fair and honest man who treated the Indians with compassion and considered them a highly civilized people. He even married an Indian woman, despite a national prejudice which frowned on such unions.

Because McKee was not willing to trick Indians into surrendering more land than was necessary, he probably secured less favorable treaty terms for the United States in 1801 and 1805 than could have been secured. When some criticized the

Choctaw War effort against the Creeks in 1814, McKee defended their participation in the conflict and their achievements on the battlefield.[20] In 1818 he served with Mississippi state Sen. Daniel Burnet and Gen. William Carroll as the United States commissioner to secure Choctaw lands at an abortive treaty negotiation. As soon as the tribesmen stated that they would not cede any land, McKee thanked them for their time and concluded the negotiations, much to the chagrin of Burnet and Carroll who wanted to pressure the Choctaws into at least a token cession.[21] The following year he served with Burnet and Andrew Jackson at another negotiation parley with the Choctaws. This time Jackson took the lead in the negotiations and did everything possible to secure a cession of land, including long harangues, threats, and dire predictions of future extermination. When the Indians held fast to their position, McKee, as Indian agent, ended the negotiations and allowed the Choctaws to break camp. McKee's fair dealing, defense of the Choctaws at the treaty site, and willingness to leave without securing one concession infuriated Jackson. He wrote a scathing letter to Calhoun, including a diatribe against John McKee because the agent liked the Choctaws and would "use no influence which he believed to be inconsistent with the interest of the [Choctaw] Nation."[22]

The point is that in no way does McKee live up to the bad press Indian agents have received; he certainly does not fit the general definition we have of these agents. And his friendship with the Choctaws did not hurt his future career; in 1822, living in Tuscaloosa County, Alabama, he won a seat in the United States House of Representatives and served three terms before retiring in 1828.

On the other hand, William Ward emerges from the source material as an insensitive, immoral, scheming agent who would do everything possible to remove and even to destroy Indians. From 1821 onward Ward devoted his life to one goal—the removal of the Choctaw Indians from Mississippi. He negotiated in bad faith, paid off treaty obligations with rotten meat and short orders of corn, flaunted governmental instructions, and even destroyed directives rather than follow them.[23] When the

Choctaw removal treaty was finally negotiated at Dancing Rabbit Creek in 1830, Ward was still not satisfied because it contained article 14 which allowed the Indians to remain behind in Mississippi on a section or more of land, if they registered with the agent within six months.[24] Ward's opposition to the possibility of tribesmen remaining behind was nothing less than violent. He was so ardent in his wish to see no Indians remain in the state that he put off registering the Choctaws as long as he could, pretending at times to be ill and occasionally going into hiding.[25] Finally, however, he reluctantly registered Choctaws out of compliance with the treaty. Even so he often managed to find some way to defraud the Indians. One Choctaw later testified in a statement of grievance:

> In the month of January, 1831, being within six months after the ratification of said treaty, a large body of Choctaw Indians attended at a council house to have their names registered for the purpose of obtaining citizenship, and acquiring reservations according to the customs of the Indians. Unacquainted with the English language, they presented to the agent a number of sticks of various lengths, indicating how many were present, and the quantities of land to which they were severally entitled, but the agent threw down the sticks. Then they selected two or three head men to speak for them, and these head men by means of an interpreter, told the agent their number, ages, and names, and demanded registration; but the agent would not register them and told them that there were too many—that they must or should go beyond the Mississippi. Many of these Indians ignorantly despairing of the justice of the United States, have reluctantly removed beyond the Mississippi.[26]

It is a great miscarriage of justice and a distortion of history to lump John McKee and William Ward together in the same group and maintain that all agents were basically similar in their goals and efforts. It makes understanding and evaluating the role they played in the story impossible. The simple fact that the Choctaws wept when McKee resigned his post and cheered when Ward was fired in 1832 is enough to indicate that a full-fledged reevaluation of Indian agents is in order.

The same is basically true with missionaries. I have read Indian histories that dismiss missionaries as narrow partisans who contributed little of significance except to mouth the goals of denominations that would use the Bible as their weapon to relieve Indians of land. Such an indictment is, of course, true in a number of cases. The Choctaw Nation had several missionaries preaching redemption and salvation through removal. But, as was the case with the military, Indian agents, and other groups not mentioned in this chapter, the indictment is too harsh and too general. Among the Choctaw Indians from 1818 onward past the removal date dwelt Cyrus Kingsbury, Cyrus Byington, and dozens of other Presbyterians and Congregationalists representing the American Board of Commissioners for Foreign Missions. The work of these people was significant. They established experimental farms at Eliot and Mayhew missions, lived Christianity rather than preached it, never maintained superiority of race and culture, and contributed what they could as individuals to the general community.[27] Kingsbury was not only successful as a missionary because of his humanity and daily life, but he also became a leader in the Choctaw Nation, advising the tribal council and individual mingoes and serving as a Choctaw commissioner and advisor at treaty negotiations.[28]

By 1830 Kingsbury, Byington, and the others in their group were so identified with Choctaws and resistance to removal that they were actually banned from the treaty grounds at Dancing Rabbit Creek by the United States commissioners John Eaton and John Coffee. Thousands of Indians were welcomed to the treaty site, along with white gamblers, saloon keepers, wanted criminals, and prostitutes,[29] but when Kingsbury and Byington arrived they were greeted by an order stipulating that all missionaries must abandon the treaty grounds by 18 September. In the order Eaton and Coffee stated that it would be "improper" for missionaries to be present because the commissioners and Indians were negotiating a treaty—not holding divine services.[30] Eaton's reasoning fooled no one, for it was well known in Mississippi that the commissioners feared the political influence of the Protestant missionaries, not their preaching. The missionaries complained bitterly about the decision but to no avail;[31] they were forced away from the treaty site by troops under the command of the United States commissioners.

Again, a general indictment does not hold true. There were fine, decent, and honest missionaries in the Choctaw country and all over the United States during the decades of white-red confrontation. There were also scamps who brought dishonor on themselves, their churches, and the nation. But they should not be lumped together any more than the various elements of all other groups should be considered as some totality. There is a dichotomy in the approaches of different people to Indians, but it is not by occupation. Rather it is between individual people who approached Indians through their own definitions of right, moral and immoral, and the general good.

Though there are other myths that need attention, the one that is most disturbing is that a majority of people who write on Indian topics apparently have little interest at all in Indians. They show no appreciation of Indian historic and cultural achievements. They judge Indians by how "white" they have become. Three words are particularly annoying—"savage," "uncivilized," and "progress." If these three words could be banished from Indian studies—or from the dictionary, for that matter—untold strides forward would have been made. For example, to many writers a savage is an Indian who is not acculturated and is still true to tribal customs and heritage. Many suggest that a civilized or good Indian is one who has become part white, at least in his practices, and is now on the way to swallowing "white culture" hook, line, and sinker. Progress to them is evident when we can get Indians to adopt white man's law, agricultural habits, dress, language, and morals. The same has been historically true in the evaluation of other minority groups. Many earlier writers ridiculed immigrants from Ireland, Poland, Italy, and other countries who got off the boat wearing strange clothes, practicing different cultural habits, and speaking another language. As they became Americanized—whatever that is—they became more acceptable to society in general. Black people, who did not want to come here in the first place, have been depicted as savages because of their illiteracy, their desire to escape the "security" of slavery, and, of course, their color. So it has been with the American Indian. He is depicted as the most savage of the savage. Why have we demanded that he give up his legal system for one that condoned stealing Indian's land and killing him? Why have we demanded that Indians give up their agricultural techniques when we are willing to admit that Indian agriculture gave the world corn, beans, and untold other foods? Why do we call Indians shiftless and lazy when we know what they have been through for over four hundred years at our hands?

The study of American Indians is fascinating, important, and rewarding. These native Americans have been discussed, lauded, persecuted, and misunderstood for centuries. However, fellow historians have preferred to study other topics that seem more glamorous and important. That is certainly their privilege, but it is encouraging to know that finally the public is really interested in solid Indian research and that scholars are flocking to the archives and reservations in search of answers to important questions that for too long were not even asked.

NOTES

1. Arthur H. DeRosier, Jr., *The Removal of the Choctaw Indians* (Knoxville: University of Tennessee Press, 1970).

2. Ora Brooks Peake, *A History of the United States Indian Factory System, 1795–1822* (Denver: Sage Books, 1954). The factory system, as it was called, was supposedly established to keep dishonest private traders from defrauding the Indians. Government-operated trading houses, or factories, were built on tribal lands, and goods were sold at moderate prices. Even more important, private traders who desired to operate among the Indians had to be licensed by the government.

3. Leland D. Baldwin, *The Stream of American History*, 2 vols. (New York: American Book, 1953), 1: 512.

4. Thomas Jefferson to William Henry Harrison, 27 February 1803, Andrew A. Lipscomb and Albert E. Bergh, eds., *The Writings of Thomas Jefferson: Memorial Edition Containing His Autobiography, Notes on*

Virginia, Parliamentary Manual, Official Papers, Messages and Addresses, and Other Writings, Official and Private, Now Collected and Published in their Entirety for the First Time, Including All of the Original Manuscripts Deposited in the Department of State and Published in 1853 by Order of the Joint Committee of Congress with Numerous Illustrations and a Comprehensive Analytical Index, 20 vols. (Washington, D.C.: Thomas Jefferson Memorial Association of the United States, 1904), 10: 370.

5. Henry Dearborn to James Wilkinson, 16 April 1803, Clarence E. Carter, ed., *The Territorial Papers of the United States,* 17 vols. (Washington, D.C.: Government Printing Office, 1937), 5: 213; Charles C. Royce, comp., "Indian Land Cessions in the United States," pt. 2 of *Eighteenth Annual Report of the Bureau of American Ethnology to the Secretary of the Smithsonian Institution, 1896–97,* ed. J. W. Powell, no. 736, 56th Cong., 1st sess. (Washington, D.C., 1899), p. 664.

6. Thomas Jefferson to M. DuPont DeNemours, 1 November 1803, Thomas Jefferson Randolph, ed., *Memoir, Correspondence, and Miscellanies, from the Papers of Thomas Jefferson,* 4 vols. (Charlottesville, Va., 1829), 4: 5–6.

7. Royce, "Indian Land Cessions," pp. 650, 662, 664.

8. John C. Calhoun to United States House of Representatives, 8 December 1818, Richard K. Cralle, ed., *Reports and Public Letters of John C. Calhoun,* 6 vols. (New York, 1888), 5: 19.

9. Walter Lowrie and Walter S. Franklin, eds., *American State Papers: Documents, Legislative, and Executive, of the Congress of the United States, from the First Session of the Fourteenth to the Second Session of the Nineteenth Congress, Inclusive: Commencing December 4, 1815, and Ending March 3, 1827,* 11 vols. (Washington, D.C., 1834), 6: 241; see also DeRosier, *Choctaw Removal,* pp. 168–172.

10. Lowrie and Franklin, *American State Papers,* 6: 238. The land ceded by the United States in the West was almost three times larger than the Mississippi land received from the Indians.

11. W. David Baird, "Arkansas's Choctaw Boundary: A Study of Justice Delayed," *Arkansas Historical Quarterly* 28 (1969): 203.

12. Ibid., pp. 204, 205.

13. Thomas Jefferson to John Breckenridge, 12 August 1803, Randolph, *Memoir,* 3: 512.

14. Royce, "Indian Land Cessions," p. 708.

15. Angie Debo, *The Rise and Fall of the Choctaw Republic,* 2d ed. (Norman: University of Oklahoma Press, 1961).

16. DeRosier, *Choctaw Removal,* pp. 133–147.

17. George Gibson to Jacob Brown, 12 April 1832, Lettterbook of Commissary General of Subsistence, Letters sent MS, Records of the Bureau of Indian Affairs, National Archives, Washington, D.C.

18. *Arkansas Gazette,* 28 December 1831 and 8 February 1832; Muriel H. Wright, "The Removal of the Choctaws to the Indian Territory," *Chronicles of Oklahoma* 6 (1928): 107.

19. *Dictionary of American Biography,* S.V. "McKee, John."

20. John McKee to Andrew Jackson, 26 January 1814, Andrew Jackson MS, Library of Congress, Washington, D.C.

21. John McKee to John C. Calhoun, 27 October 1818, Letters received

by Secretary of War, 1801–1860, War Department MS, National Archives, Washington, D.C.

22. Andrew Jackson to John C. Calhoun, 25 August 1819, Andrew Jackson MS.

23. John C. Calhoun to William Ward, 19 May 1821, Indian Affairs, Letters sent, War Department MS, National Archives, Washington, D.C.; DeRosier, *Choctaw Removal,* pp. 75–76; *Arkansas Gazette,* 7 January 1824.

24. Article 14, Treaty of Dancing Rabbit Creek, 27 September 1830, Copy of the treaty included in DeRosier, *Choctaw Removal,* pp. 174–182.

25. Choctaw Claims Journal of Commissioners Murray and Vroom; also General Deposition and a list of the Heads of Families Claiming Land under Article 14 of the Treaty of 1830 MS, Bureau of Indian Affairs, National Archives, Washington, D.C.

26. Lowrie and Franklin, *American State Papers,* 8: 432.

27. *Panopolist and Missionary Herald* (Boston) 16 (1819): 389, 509; *Missionary Herald* (Boston) 16 (1820): 80–81; Cyrus Kingsbury to Pushmataha, 6 April 1820, John McKee MS, Library of Congress, Washington, D.C.

28. *Missionary Herald* 17 (1821): 208.

29. Henry S. Halbert, "The Story of the Treaty of Dancing Rabbit," *Publications of the Mississippi Historical Society* 6 (1902): 377.

30. John Eaton and John Coffee to War Department, 15 September 1830, Unsigned Journal of Commissioners. Eaton and Coffee, 15–17 September, Ratified treaty file no. 160, Choctaw, Dancing Rabbit Creek, 27 September 1830, MS, Records of the Bureau of Indian Affairs, National Archives, Washington, D.C., p. 37.

31. John Eaton to Cyrus Kingsbury, 18 September 1830, ibid., pp. 39–40.

SOURCES CITED

Arkansas Gazette. 28 December 1831–8 February 1832.

Baird, W. David. "Arkansas's Choctaw Boundary: A Study of Justice Delayed." *Arkansas Historical Quarterly* 28 (1969): 203–222.

Baldwin, Leland D. *The Stream of American History.* Vol. 1. New York: American Book, 1953.

Carter, Clarence E., ed. *The Territorial Papers of the United States.* Vol. 5. Washington, D.C.: Government Printing Office, 1937.

Cralle, Richard K., ed. *Reports and Public Letters of John C. Calhoun.* Vol. 5. New York, 1888.

Debo, Angie. *The Rise and Fall of the Choctaw Republic,* 2d ed. Norman: University of Oklahoma Press, 1961.

DeRosier, Arthur H., Jr. *The Removal of the Choctaw Indians.* Knoxville: University of Tennessee Press, 1970.

Halbert, Henry S. "The Story of the Treaty of Dancing Rabbit." *Publications of the Mississippi Historical Society* 6 (1902): 373–402.

Lipscomb, Andrew A., and Bergh, Albert E., eds. *The Writings of Thomas Jefferson: Memorial Edition Containing his Autobiography, Notes on Virginia, Parliamentary Manual, Official Papers, Messages and Addresses, and Other Writings, Official and Private, Now Collected and Published in their Entirety for the First Time, Including All of the Original Manu-*

scripts Deposited in the Department of State and Published in 1853 by Order of the Joint Committee of Congress with Numerous Illustrations and a Comprehensive Analytical Index. Vol. 10. Washington, D.C.: Thomas Jefferson Memorial Association of the United States, 1904.

Missionary Herald 17 (1821).

Panoplist and Missionary Herald 16 (1819).

Powell, J. W., ed. *Eighteenth Annual Report of the Bureau of American Ethnology to the Secretary of the Smithsonian Institution, 1896–1897.* No. 736, 56th Cong., 1st sess. Washington, D.C., 1899.

Randolph, Thomas Jefferson, ed. *Memoir, Correspondence, and Miscellaneous from the Papers of Thomas Jefferson.* Vols. 3 and 4. Charlottesville, Va., 1829.

Washington, D.C. National Archives. Bureau of Indian Affairs. Choctaw Claims Journal of Commissioners Murray and Vroom; also General Deposition and a list of the Heads of Families Claiming Land under Article 14 of the Treaty of 1830, MSS.

———. National Archives. Bureau of Indian Affairs. Letters sent MSS., War Department.

———. Library of Congress. Andrew Jackson MSS.

———. National Archives. Records of the Bureau of Indian Affairs. Letterbook of Commissary General of Subsistence, Letters sent, MSS.

Wright, Muriel H. "The Removal of the Choctaws to the Indian Territory." *Chronicles of Oklahoma* 9 (1928): 103–128.

Louisiana Choctaw Life at the End of the Nineteenth Century

John H. Peterson, Jr.

With the removal of the bulk of the southern Indians to Oklahoma, the Indians remaining in the Southeast vanished from the pages of history. The Indians who resisted removal faded into obscurity, living in small groups, isolated from other Indian groups and from the larger non-Indian population which surrounded them. The travelers, missionaries, and government agents whose written reports provided much of the information on earlier Indian history no longer visited the remaining southeastern Indians. Not until the 1880s did local historians, antiquarians, and anthropologists become interested in surviving Indian groups. However, these writers were primarily interested in the traditional culture and early history of these groups and rarely described their existing way of life. As a result, little is known about how southern Indians adapted to life in a society dominated by whites.[1]

However, by combining the scattered information recorded by these earlier researchers, it is possible to reconstruct Indian life as it existed in the latter part of the nineteenth century. This possibility can best be demonstrated by focusing on a small group for which there is a limited corpus of published material, the Louisiana Choctaws.

The only widely known publication on the Louisiana Choctaws is David I. Bushnell's monograph on *The Choctaw of Bayou Lacomb*. This publication is largely based on materials

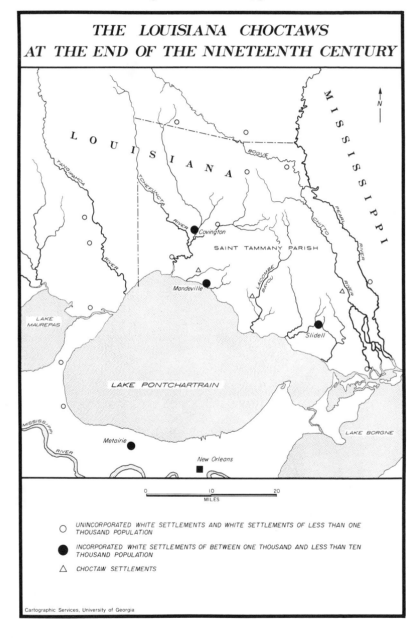

THE LOUISIANA CHOCTAWS
AT THE END OF THE NINETEENTH CENTURY

○ UNINCORPORATED WHITE SETTLEMENTS AND WHITE SETTLEMENTS OF LESS THAN ONE
    THOUSAND POPULATION

● INCORPORATED WHITE SETTLEMENTS OF BETWEEN ONE THOUSAND AND LESS THAN TEN
    THOUSAND POPULATION

△ CHOCTAW SETTLEMENTS

Cartographic Services, University of Georgia

collected by Bushnell during his visit to "lower Louisiana" from December 1908 to April 1909.[2] While Bushnell does not state how long he worked with the Choctaws, he states that "the greater part of the time was spent in St. Tammany Parish," and during "this period frequent visits were made to the few Choctaw still living near Bayou Lacomb." Bushnell notes the Choctaw population in Louisiana had been depleted only six years before his visit, when many of the remaining Choctaws were removed to Oklahoma. At the time of his visit, Bushnell found only two Choctaw settlements in Saint Tammany Parish, the one near Bayou Lacomb, which he studied, and another, which he did not visit, on the lower Pearl River.

The best single source supplementing Bushnell's information is a privately printed essay by C. Bremer entitled *The Chata Indians of Pearl River*.[3] Writing at about the same time as Bushnell, Bremer concentrates almost entirely on the second Choctaw settlement at Pearl River. Unlike Bushnell, Bremer was a permanent resident of the area and knew members of this Choctaw group for an extended period. Internal evidence is the only means for judging Bremer's reliability as an observer or for judging the similarity of the two Choctaw groups to each other. By this standard, the two groups are almost identical, and Bremer must be judged an accurate observer since her information is completely in accord with almost everything Bushnell reports as well as that of other authorities on Choctaw life.

In addition to Bremer's essay, valuable supportive information can be found in the reports of H. S. Halbert to the state superintendent of public education for the state of Mississippi for the decade 1890 to 1900. Halbert's reliability can be judged from his widely known writings on Choctaw traditional culture which are quoted at length by Swanton,[4] with whom he worked in editing Byington's dictionary.[5] Interestingly enough, with the exception of these school reports, Halbert's published material on the Choctaws focuses on traditional culture just as does the study by Bushnell. Only in these long ignored school reports do we find information about the life of the Choctaws of the upper Pearl River with whom Halbert lived for several years, serving as the first white instructor in Choctaw schools since 1830. As with Bremer, the question of the applicability of Halbert's observations in the upper Pearl River communities to Bushnell's at Bayou Lacomb must be raised. Again, judgment must be based on internal evidence, and here we find that when treating similar material, Halbert's observations are completely in accord with those of both Bremer and Bushnell. Only one major difference can be found, and this will be discussed later. Thus, it seems appropriate to utilize both Bremer and to a lesser extent Halbert in conjunction with Bushnell in reconstructing aspects of Louisiana Choctaw life around the turn of the century that were ignored or slighted by Bushnell. These aspects include social organization, subsistence economy, and intergroup relations.

Bushnell does not attempt to describe Choctaw social organization as it existed at the time of his visit. Rather he presents fragmented information on existing Choctaw settlements, surviving traditional subgroupings of the Choctaw tribe, and traditional ceremonies, without attempting to portray a viable, functioning social system. By comparing the writings of Bushnell, Halbert, and Bremer, the following pattern of Choctaw social organization at the turn of the century emerges.

Bremer describes the Louisiana Choctaw family as consisting of "a father and mother, eight to ten children, aged grandparents, and an orphan of either sex."[6] She indicates that this family was the basic subsistence unit of Choctaw society. Related families were grouped into bands which correspond to the settlements named by Bushnell[7] and the communities identified by Halbert.[8] It can be inferred from both Bushnell and Halbert that most of these locality groupings bore the name of a traditional Choctaw clan or geographic division. Halbert, on occasion, even uses the terms *community* and *clan* interchangeably.[9] Bushnell states that these localized clans were the basic exogamous unit of Choctaw society.

Before the 1903 removal, there were seven such units in Louisiana and a larger number in the upper Pearl River Valley. However, four of the Louisiana Choctaw settlements and many of the upper Pearl River settlements were removed

to Oklahoma in 1903. Bushnell describes the settlement at
Bayou Lacomb as numbering over one hundred individuals
before the 1903 removal.[10] While neither Halbert nor Bremer
mentions the numerical size of Choctaw communities they describe, Wade describes a Choctaw community in the upper
Pearl River Valley as consisting of "a few hundred people."[11]

According to Bushnell, the oldest male member of each of
these units was the recognized leader of that division of the
Choctaw people.[12] "These leaders were the ones to be consulted
whenever advice was required, and they played an important
part in arranging marriages between members of these exogamous settlements." Although Bremer does not specifically
mention the role of these settlement leaders in arranging
marriages, as does Bushnell, she does indicate that they acted
individually and in concert in advising individuals of their
groups. She further states that these leaders met at an annual
Spring Council at a specified location to discuss the general
affairs affecting the well-being of the Louisiana Choctaws. The
annual Spring Council is not mentioned by either Bushnell or
Halbert. However, a resident of New Orleans mentions attend-
ing around 1896 "one of the last tribal meetings and gatherings of the Indians who lived in St. Tammany Parish near
Bayou Lacomb."[13] He indicates that these Louisiana Choctaws
"had invited to their powwow representatives from the remnants of tribes in Mississippi and in Alabama." This not only
provides support for Bremer, but it is also the only documentary evidence of the maintenance of contacts between geo-
graphically separated Indian groups in the Deep South. During
my own fieldwork among the Mississippi Choctaws, I learned
that at least until the Second World War there were periodic
visits between Choctaws of the lower and upper Pearl River
and some intermarriage between these two groups.

One can conclude from Bushnell, Halbert, and Bremer that
the Louisiana Choctaws around the turn of the century were
organized into several exogamous settlements of related families bearing names of traditional Choctaw clans or geographic
names. Within each settlement there was an acknowledged
leader who both advised members of the settlement and met

with leaders of other settlements in an annual Spring Council to consider the affairs of the Choctaw people as a whole. Additionally, some contact was maintained with members of other Indian groups in the Deep South.

The basic manner in which the Louisiana Choctaws maintained their livelihood was ignored by Bushnell in his monograph.[14] In this work he concentrated almost entirely on utilization of wild foods and traditional methods of food preparation. Four wild plants and several wild fruits were utilized, as well as corn and rice; however, Bushnell makes no mention of cultivation. He does mention the availability of wild game but implied that it had become less abundant than formerly. He mentions the use of pork only to say that it was cooked in the traditional manner. Bushnell mentions only two sources of monetary income for the Choctaws: making of filé from sassafras leaves[15] and selling baskets. At a later date, Bushnell wrote a short informal essay which largely summarized material from his earlier publication. Only one new item of information was added: "Several vegetables were raised in gardens, among these was a variety of corn.[16] It seems significant that this item of contemporary life was not thought noteworthy for his major professional publication, but it was of interest for an informal essay.

The more pragmatic Bremer gives a great deal of insight into the subsistence economy of the Louisiana Choctaws.[17] She confirms the food items mentioned by Bushnell and mentions additionally cabbage fields, household flocks of chickens, and hogs which fattened on the open range. She also indicated that hunting remained very important. Bremer confirms the importance of the sale of filé and baskets for the Choctaw economy, but adds trapping during the winter and alligator hunting during the summer as means through which men contributed to the monetary income. Additionally, Bremer records wage labor by the Choctaw men who "crowd around the timber camps, sometimes cutting down trees . . . sometimes logging them . . . . Others build the quaint little cabins made of split boards and puncheon flooring." Bremer ascribes the economic activities followed by the Choctaw men as resulting from "doing what is yet in sympathy with their temperaments and love of nature." It seems more likely that they were engaging in economic activities which brought them into minimum contact with non-Indians or which involved their undertaking manual labor for whites. While this possibility is not supported by the descriptions of the Louisiana Choctaws at the end of the nineteenth century, it is suggested by Rouquettes' earlier description of the Louisiana Choctaws in the 1840s. Rouquette states that Choctaw men refused to undertake manual work for whites stating that they were not slaves.[18] At this time, hunting was the primary occupation of the Choctaw men, although a few would reluctantly cut and haul wood for whites. It is possible that the decline in availability of wild game mentioned by Bushnell was partially responsible for the greater willingness of Choctaw men to work in timber camps by the end of the nineteenth century.

Bremer also provides important information on the economic basis for the yearly cycle of activities for the Louisiana Choctaws.[19] She mentions a seasonal round of activities which involved the entire household. The Spring Council took place during the periods of high floodwaters in the early spring when trapping was poor, logging operations ceased, and timber camp workers were employed in floating logs to market. During this time the Choctaws collected on high ground in swampy areas where floodwaters forced game animals to concentrate, making hunting easier. Summer brought a return migration to small settlements along the edge of the swamps where crops were planted and work for the timber camps could be resumed. September, following the gathering of the "small harvests of the summer," was the time for marriages. A final gathering before the winter dispersal of population occurred on the first of November, All Saint's Day. As Catholic converts, the Choctaws held "family reunions" on this day, decorating graves and keeping candles burning throughout the day. After this, hunting, trapping, and timber work continued in importance until the spring floods again brought about a population concentration for the Spring Council. Bremer seems to suggest that each family moved through this cycle independently; however, from Bushnell's identification of established settlements made up of exogamous kinship groups, we may assume that the established settlement provided a base of operations for these extended hunting, trapping, or working expeditions.

Halbert provides additional insight into the economic basis for this seasonal pattern as it operated among the Choctaws in the upper Pearl River Valley. Here, as among the Choctaws of Louisiana, winter was the time for a seminomadic population dispersal.

> They say that by this plan, they can economize their household expenses, the men hunting and the women making and selling baskets, the proceeds from all of which supplies them with food during the winter, while their corn, pease [sic] and potatoes remain under the charge of a friend or a relative undiminished and undisturbed at home. On their return, at the close of the winter, they find their supply of home provender, of course, untouched and sufficient to help them to raise their coming crop.[20]

Halbert indicates that this practice was limited to only a few localities in the upper Pearl River by 1895, although it was probably a more general pattern that had recently declined as increasing numbers of Mississippi Choctaws entered the sharecropping system after 1880.[21] This economic pattern continued to be important in Louisiana because better hunting prevailed and there was more land available for farming by nonlandowners.

The discussion thus far has already pointed out certain aspects of intergroup relations ignored by Bushnell. The spring and fall gatherings of Louisiana Choctaws has been mentioned as well as the participation, at least on occasions, of other Indian groups from Mississippi and Alabama. It remains for us to note the relations between Choctaws and non-Choctaws. The Choctaws were already partially integrated into a market economy, selling filé and other herbs, baskets, and animal skins, as well as participating in some wage labor in timber camps. In turn, they purchased items they needed, including cooking pots, rifles, traps, clothing, rice, coffee, and whiskey.

Their way of life, however, must have minimized contact with both Negroes and whites. Bremer states: "The color line is vigorously drawn; a woman who mates with a Negro is an outcast forever. Marriage or any alliance with the Whites is not desired, but is condoned."[22] In turn, the Choctaws were given at least token white status, since Bremer states that they rode in "White-only" railroad coaches on their way to market towns. Nevertheless, the Choctaws' isolation was breaking down by the turn of the century.

> The knowledge of these [traditional] things is not passing on to the new generation of girls, who are all anxious to learn what the Whites learn thereby losing interest in their tribal arts and customs; . . . one sees them wearing shoes and corsets many sizes too small which some unscrupulous storekeeper has foisted upon them. The parents of this generation of young people are all anxious that their sons and daughters have an education, insofar as they understand the subject; only one stipulation is made; their children must attend White schools, no education being worth the humiliation of being forced to affiliate with Negroes.[23]

My purpose here has been to supplement Bushnell's classical report on the Louisiana Choctaws with additional material, thus shedding some light on the way of life of these people at the time Bushnell conducted his study. We have seen that these remaining Indians found an economic niche which permitted their survival as a people long after the disruption of removal and massive white settlement. It was this economic niche which made possible the persistence of "many of their primitive manners, customs, and beliefs."[24] However, at the time of Bushnell's study, knowledge of traditional ways was passing away as the younger generation turned to education.

NOTES

1. Murray Wax has suggested that just as the postremoval history of the southeastern Indians has been ignored, so has the poststatehood history of Indians in Oklahoma been neglected. The lack of interest in both cases

seems to stem from an unwillingness to deal with the Indian as an ethnic group in the larger society. This paper is part of a larger research plan dealing with this problem as outlined in John H. Peterson, Jr., "The Indian in the Old South," in *Red, White, and Black: Symposium on Indians in the Old South*, ed. Charles M. Hudson (Athens: University of Georgia Press, 1971), p. 130. The author's research on Choctaw history has been supported by a Phelps-Stokes Fellowship, University of Georgia, and the Social Science Research Center, Mississippi State University. Location research and original drafting of the map was undertaken by Mike Wall. The author is indebted to Charles Hudson and Robert I. Gilbert for their critical comments on this paper.

2. David I. Bushnell, Jr., *The Choctaw of Bayou Lacomb, St. Tammany Parish, Louisiana*, Smithsonian Institution, Bureau of American Ethnology Bulletin no. 48 (Washington, D.C., 1909), pp. v, 1–3.

3. C. Bremer, *The Chata Indians of Pearl River* (New Orleans: Picayune Job Print, ca. 1907). Other than statements contained within this publication, no information is available about C. Bremer. It seems probable that the author was the Miss Cora Bremer who donated Louisiana Choctaw material to the American Museum of Natural History, New York, in 1902.

4. John R. Swanton, *Source Material for the Social and Ceremonial Life of the Choctaw Indians*, Smithsonian Institution, Bureau of American Ethnology Bulletin no. 103 (Washington, D.C., 1931).

5. John R. Swanton and H. S. Halbert, eds., *A Dictionary of the Choctaw Language by Cyrus Byington*, Smithsonian Institution, Bureau of American Ethnology Bulletin no. 46 (Washington, D.C., 1915).

6. Bremer, *The Chata Indians*, p. 1.

7. Bushnell, *The Choctaw of Bayou Lacomb*, pp. 1, 16.

8. H. S. Halbert, "The Indians in Mississippi and Their Schools," *Biennial Report of the Superintendent of Public Instruction to the Legislature of Mississippi for the Scholastic Years 1893–1894 and 1894–1895* (Jackson: Clarion Ledger Publishing, 1896), pp. 535–537.

9. I have elsewhere described the breakdown of traditional moiety, clan, and geographical distinctions resulting in local groups being identified by names earlier applied to any one of these traditional units. John H. Peterson, Jr., "The Mississippi Band of Choctaw Indians: Their Recent History and Current Social Relations (Ph.D. diss., University of Georgia, 1970), pp. 145–146.

10. Bushnell, *The Choctaw of Bayou Lacomb*, p. 3.

11. John W. Wade, "The Removal of the Mississippi Choctaw," *Publications of the Mississippi Historical Society*, (Oxford, Miss.: Printed for the Society, 1904), p. 401.

12. Bushnell, *The Choctaw of Bayou Lacomb*, p. 16.

13. Andre La Farge, "Louisiana Linguistics and Folklore Backgrounds," *Louisiana Historical Quarterly* 24 (1941): 744–755.

14. Bushnell, *The Choctaw of Bayou Lacomb*, pp. 8–10, 13.

15. Filé is a powder made from young leaves of sassafras and used to flavor and thicken soups and stews. Use of this herb was adopted from the Choctaws by the French in Louisiana and has come to be most closely identified with Creole cooking. Filé is still sold commercially in Louisiana under such names as Creole Gumbo Filé. The modern version may contain in addition to sassafras leaves a smaller proportion of thyme leaves.

16. David I. Bushnell, Jr., "The Choctaw of St. Tammany Parish," *Louisiana Historical Quarterly* 1 (1917): 14.

17. Bremer, *The Chata Indians*, pp. 1–2, 8, 10–11.

18. Dominique Rouquette, "The Choctaws" (typescript translation by Olivia Blanehard, Louisiana State Museum Library, New Orleans, 1938), pp. 12–14.

19. Bremer, *The Chata Indians*, pp. 1–2, 9. Published after this article was prepared for publication, the following work provides valuable confirmation of the Choctaw annual cycle as described by Bremer: Bob F. Perkins, ed., *Geoscience and Man* (Baton Rouge: School of Geoscience, Louisiana State University, 1972), vol. 2, *Atchafalaya Swamp Life, Settlement, and Folk Occupations*, by Malcolm L. Comeaux. Although the Atchafalaya Swamp dwellers are white, their hunting, fishing, and lumbering economy around the turn of the century closely paralleled the Louisiana Choctaw economy. The major difference was that, unlike the Choctaw, the swamp dwellers did not engage in agriculture during the summer months.

20. Halbert, "The Indians in Mississippi," p. 539.

21. Peterson, "The Mississippi Band of Choctaw Indians," p. 58.

22. Bremer, *The Chata Indians*, p. 4.

23. Ibid., p. 8.

24. Bushnell, "The Choctaw of St. Tammany Parish," p. 12.

SOURCES CITED

Bremer, C. *The Chata Indians of Pearl River*. New Orleans: Picayune Job Print, ca. 1907.

Bushnell, David I., Jr. *The Choctaw of Bayou Lacomb, St. Tammany Parish, Louisiana*. Smithsonian Institution. Bureau of American Ethnology Bulletin no. 48. Washington, D.C., 1909.

———. "The Choctaw of St. Tammany Parish." *Louisiana Historical Quarterly* 1 1917): 11–20.

Halbert, H. S. "The Indians in Mississippi and Their Schools." *Biennial Report of the Superintendent of Public Instruction to the Legislature of Mississippi for the Scholastic Years 1893–1894 and 1894–1895*. Jackson: Clarion Ledger Publishing, 1896, pp. 534–545.

La Farge, Andre. "Louisiana Linguistics and Folklore Backgrounds." *Louisiana Historical Quarterly* 24 (1941): 744–55.

Peterson, John H., Jr. "The Mississippi Band of Choctaw Indians: Their Recent History and Current Social Relations." Ph.D. dissertation, University of Georgia, 1970.

———. "The Indian in the Old South." In *Red, White, and Black: Symposium on Indians in the Old South*, edited by Charles M. Hudson, pp. 116–134. Athens: University of Georgia Press, 1971.

Rouquette, Dominique. "The Choctaws." Typescript translation by Olivia Blanehard, Louisiana State Museum Library, New Orleans, 1938.

Swanton, John R. *Source Material for the Social and Ceremonial Life of the Choctaw Indians*. Smithsonian Institution. Bureau of American Ethnology Bulletin no. 103. Washington, D.C., 1931.

———, and Halbert, H. S., eds., *A Dictionary of the Choctaw Language, by*

Cyrus Byington. Smithsonian Institution. Bureau of American Ethnology Bulletin no. 46. Washington, D.C., 1915.

Wade, John W. "The Removal of the Mississippi Choctaw." *Publications of the Mississippi Historical Society*. Oxford, Miss.: Printed for the Society, 1904, pp. 397–426.

An Analysis of Cherokee Sorcery and Witchcraft[1]

Raymond D. Fogelson

The aboriginality of Cherokee sorcery and witchcraft beliefs and practices seems assured from comparative ethnological data, linguistic evidence, and the degree of elaboration encountered in the period when reliable ethnographic material becomes available. Several early colonial documents contain occasional allusive references to conjurers and witches. One of the earliest concise descriptions of Cherokee beliefs in this area is found in Judge John Haywood's *Natural and Aboriginal History of Tennessee*, published in 1823. Haywood notes:

> In ancient times the Cherokees had no conception of any one's dying a natural death. They universally ascribed the death of those who perished by disease to the intervention or agency of evil spirits, and witches, and conjurers, who had connexion with the Shina [Hebraic evil being], or evil spirits. They ascribe to their witches and conjurers the power to put on any shape they please, either of bird, or beast, but they are supposed generally to prefer the form of a cat or of an owl. They ascribe to them the power of passing from one place to another in as short a time as they please. . . . Their witches and conjurers are supposed to receive their faculties from evil spirits, and are punished to this day with death. Suspicion affixes to them the imputation of this crime. A person dying by disease, and charging his death to have been procured by means of witchcraft, or spirits, by any other person, consigns that person to inevitable death. They profess to believe that their conjurations have no effect on white men.[2]

That Cherokee witchcraft was a living reality rather than empty superstition is attested to by the fact that in 1824 the Arkansas Cherokees enacted legislation making it a capital offense to murder a suspected witch. In addition merely accusing someone of practicing witchcraft was punishable by whipping.[3]

Cherokee sorcery and witchcraft beliefs and practices have been studied and restudied for over eighty years by anthropologists. Despite this continuous effort, there is still no comprehensive picture of this complex subject.

James Mooney initiated modern anthropological studies of Cherokee medicomagical knowledge through his discovery of the existence of native texts, written in the Sequoyah syllabary.[4] These texts, called "sacred formulas" by Mooney, were owned by native practitioners and formed the basis of Cherokee medicomagical philosophy and practice. The writing down of this material imbued it with tangibility and an aura of sanctity that insured a fairly literal transmission of the knowledge contained within these texts. It is known that Sequoyah created his syllabary in the 1820s and that his invention diffused rapidly throughout the Cherokee Nation, penetrating even culturally conservative pockets of the preremoval population where English was scarcely known and the inroads of acculturation had not yet seriously undermined the traditional belief structure. Much of the ritual knowledge contained in these texts appears to have been set down in the decades immediately preceding and following the Cherokee removal in 1838. Indirect evidence for this assumption lies in the frequent "archaisms" that bedevil anyone, even a fluent contemporary Cherokee speaker, who attempts to translate these texts. If we assume that these texts were originally recorded by tribal elders, with whom such knowledge traditionally resides, then the provenience of this material can, perhaps, be extended back to the end of the eighteenth century. These "sacred formulas" contain instructions and rituals for curing, preventing, or transmitting a multitude of culturally recognized disease entities. In addition a large number of texts deal with love magic, with various forms of divination, with special rituals for the ballgame and warfare, and with a whole host of additional subjects.[5]

In *The Sacred Formulas of the Cherokee* (1891) Mooney presented a brief synopsis of beliefs and practice with regard to medicine and disease, as well as translations of twenty-eight specimen texts, including six dealing with love magic, two to prevent sorcery and witchcraft, and one "to destroy life." Mooney collected several hundred additional sacred formulas —or *idi:gawé:sdi* ("things said") to use the more appropriate Cherokee name.[6] These were deposited and remain in the Smithsonian Institution archives.

Mooney's pioneering work was extended and elaborated after his death by the Belgian anthropologist Frans Olbrechts. Olbrechts spent a year with the North Carolina Cherokees where he re-collected, reedited, and retranslated a collection of medical *idi:gawé:sdi* once belonging to A.yûn.i ("Swimmer"), one of Mooney's major informants. The product of Olbrechts's dedicated labors was *The Swimmer Manuscript*,[7] which, besides containing translations of ninety-eight medical *idi:gawé:-sdi*, includes a detailed introduction to Cherokee medico-magical beliefs. With the passing of so many knowledgeable curing specialists in recent decades, the information contained in *The Swimmer Manuscript* can be obtained from no other source today. The richness and uniqueness of the material plus the ethnographic and linguistic skills of Mooney and Olbrechts combine to make *The Swimmer Manuscript* probably the best study of ethnomedicine available for any North American Indian society. It is surprising with the present levels of interest in medical anthropology and native belief systems at an all-time high that the value of this monograph has scarcely been appreciated by other than Cherokee specialists.

During the 1940s Frank Speck and John Witthoft collected important information on Cherokee ceremonialism and beliefs.[8] Much of their material dealing with medicine and magic, including a considerable number of *idi:gawé:sdi* once belonging to Will West Long, has not seen the light of published day but is available for study in the library of the

American Philosophical Society. In the late 1950s I collected information on changing medicomagical beliefs and ballgame ritualism.[9] While I did not focus directly on the subjects of sorcery and witchcraft, a certain amount of data on these topics was obtained during the course of fieldwork.

More recently Jack and Anna Kilpatrick, two gifted Cherokee scholars with a remarkable grasp of the subtleties of written and spoken Cherokee, undertook long overdue work among the Oklahoma Cherokees, as well as translating and editing some of the manuscripts collected by Mooney and Olbrechts in North Carolina. The Kilpatricks succeeded in collecting, translating, and publishing a number of *idi:gawé:-sdi* in numerous papers[10] and in three important monographs: *Walk in Your Soul*, devoted to the topic of Cherokee love magic; *Run toward the Nightland*, a general treatment of the wide range of Cherokee magic; and a recently published monograph *Notebook of a Cherokee Shaman*,[11] a collection of fifty *idi:gawé:sdi*. The Oklahoma material is especially crucial in revealing continuities and changes in belief structure as the Western Cherokees adapted to a new ecological and social situation.

The present analysis is a preliminary attempt to comprehend some aspects of the larger structure of Cherokee witchcraft and sorcery beliefs by examining culturally recognized categories of witches and sorcerers. This study is synthetic in combining documentary sources with information gathered from informants, in considering both North Carolina and Oklahoma Cherokees, and in not adhering to a specific synchronic level. The treatment is qualitative and inferential, rather than quantitative and firmly documented as is the case, for example, in Kluckhohn's study of *Navaho Witchcraft*.[12] The arguments and generalizations offered here are not buttressed by a substantial collection of case histories. Rather, this work is an attempt to put in order some facts and speculations about Cherokee sorcery and witchcraft, to place the Cherokee data in perspective relative to comparable beliefs and practices in other societies, and to advance some generalizations about that data which can hopefully direct more specific investigations in the field and in the library, especially through analysis of the rich treasure of translated and untranslated *idi:gawé:sdi.*

For purposes of this essay, sorcery and witchcraft may collectively be defined as the presumed ability of one human being to effect, directly or indirectly, undesirable transformations of state in another human being. The ability to induce adverse changes of state in another person directly through innate capacities, as acts of an inherently evil or maleficent disposition, is generally ascribed to the realm of witchcraft. Witches in many societies are thought to derive their powers through some form of putative biological inheritance. Sorcery, in contrast, usually refers to acquired knowledge of specific incantations and ritual acts that enable a practitioner to invoke spiritual agents or occult forces for the purpose of causing misfortune, illfare, or even death to a designated victim.

Another way of conceptualizing traditional distinctions between witchcraft and sorcery is to employ the familiar philosophic antithesis between nature and culture, a mode of analysis that dates back at least to the pre-Socratic philosophers and is enjoying renewed vogue through the stimulating logical exercises of Claude Lévi-Strauss. Witchcraft, though perhaps conceived of as unnatural or abnormal from a psychosocial point of view, nevertheless can be thought of as natural in being genetically or ontogenetically grounded and as a fact of nature in the sense of being uncontrolled and relatively uncontrollable by available human cultural resources. Sorcery, as an acquired or learned technique, is clearly a product of human cultural evolution. As such, sorcery is subject to various sociocultural control systems. A sorcerer can decide whether, when, and in what way to employ his magical procedures. Also, as is well known, he can decide to terminate these procedures under certain circumstances. Witchcraft, as an avowedly contracultural and antisocial activity, lacks most of these control features. Other distinctions seem to follow from the nature-culture opposition. Witchcraft tends to have a quality of directness in that the witch generally works to achieve his or her ends without the use of intermediate instrumental spiritual beings or without mechanical or technological devices. Sometimes a witch can influence events by mystical teleportation; more often a witch must make direct contact with the victim, usually in metamorphosed form. This latter requirement can prove to be something of a liability, since it may make the witch vulnerable to the elaborate antiwitchcraft procedures capable of being mobilized in many cultures. The directness-indirectness dimension can also be seen in the fact that witchcraft typically involves a simple two-party interaction between witch and victim, while sorcery usually involves three- and four-party interactions composed of sorcerer or sorcerers, client or clients, and victim.

While the intended effects of witchcraft and sorcery practices are often indistinguishable (i.e., both can cause identical undesirable transformations of state in a person), the two phenomena can usually be distinguished in terms of process. It is generally held that one can study witchcraft *beliefs*, but not witchcraft *procedures*. Witchcraft is regarded as eventuating from mental acts of will involving immanent powers not amenable to empirical observation. The process of sorcery, on the other hand, may be studied more directly, since the utilization of spells, curses, incantations, and ritual action generally takes the form of externalized observable magical procedures. Sorcery techniques follow a definite system of logic that can often be approached through native exegesis. To put the matter simply, it is possible to become a sorcerer's apprentice, but tutelage from a witch is, at least, pedagogically problematic.

The now traditional anthropological distinction between sorcery and witchcraft was, of course, originally formulated by E. E. Evans-Pritchard to accommodate his Zande data.[13] The distinction rapidly became generalized to a near universal by enshrinement in most introductory anthropology textbooks. Its influence was profoundly felt as anthropologists consciously or unconsciously forced their data to fit this dichotomous mold. Such recent work as the volume edited by Middleton and Winter on *Witchcraft and Sorcery in East Africa*,[14] Victor Turner's critical review of this work,[15] the volume on witchcraft confessions and accusations edited by Mary Douglas,[16] and the collection of papers edited by Deward Walker entitled *Systems of North American Witchcraft and Sorcery*[17] all point to the analytic limitations of the sorcery-witchcraft dichotomy and implicitly argue for more careful descriptions of such belief and action systems in the particular society's *own* terms before attempting premature cross-cultural comparison and generalization. As this study demonstrates, the sorcerer-witch distinction has only partial applicability in interpreting the Cherokee data.

Understanding of the various categories of persons who the Cherokees believe are capable of effecting adverse transformations of state in other individuals is made difficult by the coexistence, but frequent nonidentity, of native and English terms of reference. Many of the native terms today defy precise definition, and informants often disagree about the amount of semantic space occupied by analogous English terms.

We will begin by discussing those types of individuals whom contemporary Cherokees refer to by the English term *witch*. The two principal defining criteria of Cherokee "witches" appear to be a capacity for metamorphosis and an inherently evil disposition. Although witches are believed to possess powers of clairvoyance and can effect their wicked ends by omnipotence of thought (e.g., they can read people's minds and make someone sick merely by wishing him so), the evidence suggests that Cherokee witches more commonly accomplish their nefarious designs by changing their form and making direct physical contact with their victims. The most frequently reported forms of metamorphosis include ravens, owls, cats, balls of fire, shafts of purplish light, and other human beings, including those of the opposite sex. Witches can also make themselves invisible to normal sight, although special herbal decoctions can be taken by men and dogs to detect their presence.

With respect to inherent evil, the second defining attribute of a witch, the Cherokees feel that witches are irredeemable beings whose true existence falls outside the realm of humanity. Whereas a basically humane person (*u:dáno:ti*, "a man of soul, heart, feeling") may commit an unjust act out of weakness, understandable provocation, or error, his actions may be

forgiven, and in the past the Cherokees had many institutionalized forms of redemption and reconciliation. However, a
wrong committed by an acknowledged or suspected witch can
never be condoned, since such behavior represents unmitigated
malice. Witches are believed to prey on human communities
by adding the unexpired normal life expectancies of their
victims to their own. As a result older people are increasingly
suspected of practicing witchcraft with advancing age. Old age
in Cherokee society is associated with power, and the implied
power commands deference by others. The traditional Cherokee tendency to defer to older persons is sometimes regarded
in terms of honor or love, as exemplified in the Cherokee
political category of "beloved old men." However, this usage
may be a euphemistic secondary rationalization, with the
underlying psychodynamic root of this deferential behavior
being fear of the power of elders. Relief from the depredations
of a witch is only accomplished through his or her—or perhaps
more appropriately its—death.

The Cherokees employ at least three nonmutually exclusive
terms that correspond roughly to the general conception of a
witch. One term, *tsi:kili*, literally means "hoot owl," a bird of
ill omen who supposedly performs its maleficent activities at
night.[18] A second appellation given to witches, *suna:yi aneda'i*,
can be translated "they walk about during the night" or, more
simply, "night walkers." Both of these terms reflect the wide-
spread belief that witches have an affinity for darkness and
that most of their activities take place under nocturnal cover.

A third term that nudges into a portion of the semantic
space occupied by the Cherokee notion of witch is *ada:wé:hi*, a
word defying precise translation but sometimes rendered as
"wizard," suggesting a composite witch-sorcerer category. This
term is very frequently used to flatter a wide variety of spiritual
beings in the written *idi:gawé:sdi*, but can also be applied to
a human magical practitioner who has, to use Olbrechts's apt
phrase "got the utmost."[19] The Kilpatricks despairingly note
that this term has indiscriminately been equated with "medicine man" by non-Cherokee writers; they comment that "the
chances of the average Roman Catholic for achieving canoni-
zation are far greater than those of a Cherokee medicine man

for ever being considered an *ada:wé:hi*."[20] Most contemporary Eastern Cherokees would readily agree that there are no *ani:-da:wé:hi* (plural form) among them today, although there is a hesternalgic tendency to confer such exalted status on bygone practitioners whose reputed feats become more fantastically exaggerated with the passage of time.[21]

Unlike traditional Western European belief, a Cherokee witch may be either male or female and given the mechanism of metamorphosis can be both at different times. Field data and the small amount of available literature indicate no proclivity for male or female predominance in supposed witchcraft activity. Theoretically, the status of witch is not considered to be limited to a specific age. However, as discussed previously, older people are more likely to be suspected of witchcraft than younger adults or children.

Additional insight into Cherokee conceptions of witches can be derived by examining the processes by which an individual is thought to become a witch. Although witches are described as having an inherent propensity for evil, the Cherokees do not believe such characteristics to be prenatally determined as part of a genetic or "blood" inheritance.

Olbrechts reports a procedure thought to produce witches that involves a special twenty-four day regimen imposed on infants, particularly on twins. During this period the infant is denied the mother's or any other woman's breast, subsists on liquid from fermented hominy given him only at night, and is kept strictly concealed from any visitors.[22] Data obtained by Charles Holzinger in 1957[23] provide basic confirmation of Olbrechts's information, although many details vary. Holzinger was told that with parental consent an infant could be made into a witch with the aid of a conjurer. The infant is isolated from the mother's breast for seven days and nourished on a specially decocted herbal tea. According to informant testimony:

> The first born child is fed on tea for seven days before it sucks titties. Just the mother, daddy, and conjurer are allowed to see the baby. It's got too much power, like the ravens it can go over everything's head. It can look right through a house or a woman's dress. It can tell just by

looking what you're going to say. If they do only part of it [i.e., terminate the ritual before the full seven days], it can crawl like a possum, but if it's the seven days, it can fly.

Olbrechts notes precocity in youngsters subjected to such treatment.[24] Besides being able to metamorphose themselves into various human and animal forms, they gratify their needs through omnipotence of thought and also can communicate and play with the "Little People," a class of mischievous, childlike spiritual beings who are normally invisible to ordinary human eyes. If other members of the community discover that someone is planning to raise a witch child, they can abort the process by slipping some food prepared by a menstruating woman into the diet of the secluded infant. If indeed these beliefs bear any relationship to actual practice, it is difficult to understand possible reasons why any Cherokee parent would voluntarily choose to have his child raised as a witch. While it *is* believed that children so reared are self-sufficient, with boys able to become unfailing hunters and girls able to accomplish domestic tasks through powers of thought, nevertheless such individuals become disturbing elements in the ongoing functioning of society. As Olbrechts notes, "When they are grown up they are most annoying individuals; they always know what you think, and you could not possibly mislead them. And what is worse, they can make you ill, dejected, lovesick, dying, merely by thinking you in such a condition."[25] Moreover, a suspected witch's life is in chronic jeopardy, since an elaborate array of counterwitchcraft measures may be deployed by an outraged community.

Another method by which an individual can be made into a witch at a later age is recognized by the Cherokees. This involves a fast and the drinking of a decoction of a rare plant, which Olbrechts tentatively identifies as *Saggittaria latifolia* Willd., said to resemble a beetlelike insect, with the stem of the plant growing through its mouth. If the infusion is drunk and the fast maintained for four consecutive days, the individual is believed to attain the capacity for metamorphosis into creatures living on the surface of the ground. However, if the ritual is continued for seven days, the individual is thought to be capable of transformation into various kinds of flying creatures and to be able to travel underground in the manner of a mole or an earthworm.[26] One of the more common forms of metamorphosis for those undergoing the seven-day treatment was transformation into a raven; such a witch was designated *kà:lo:na a:yéli:ski* or "Raven Mocker." This type of witch probably bears relationship to the ancient Cherokee war title of "Raven," a position whose duties entailed scouting the enemy at night. My informant recognized the procedures just described but was unable to shed further light on the identification of the mysterious plant mentioned by Olbrechts.

We now come to the Cherokee category most closely approximating the anthropological usage of the term *sorcerer*. The Cherokees do not use the English term *sorcerer*,[27] but instead use the term *conjurer*, which survives from colonial days, as a gloss for what we would consider a practitioner of sorcery. The word *conjuring* for some Cherokees encompasses the whole range of positive and negative magic and varieties of divination. For others, conjuring connotes only or primarily harmful forms of coercive magic. In point of fact it is often difficult to classify a given instance as positive or negative magic or more popularly as "white" or "black magic." For instance, in cases of love magic in which a deserted wife and mother solicits the services of a conjurer to get back her absent husband, the rituals may have a happy or positive result in reuniting the family, but the errant husband has nonetheless been a victim of sorcery.

At least three terms occur that may or may not designate different types of sorcery practitioners. The first term *didá:hnese:-sgi* is the generic reference for sorcerer, occurring both in Oklahoma[28] and in North Carolina.[29] Olbrechts despairs of analyzing the etymology of the term, except to suggest that it may have some connection with the verb *to droop*; he translates the word as "man-killer." The Kilpatricks provide the literal meaning of the term as "putter-in and drawer-out of them, he," which doubtless refers to the sorcerer's magical introjection of objects or minute animate beings into the victim, as well as the removal of vital substances or organs from the victim's body.

The Kilpatricks recognize the belief in a specific class of malevolent practitioner called *ané:li:sgi*, translated as "those who think purposefully"[30] or, more simply, "thinkers,"[31] euphemisms for "anti-social human beings who, through the power of mind, project evil upon other human beings." The Kilpatricks further remark that, "an animal or bird spirit may be the actual missile, but it was loosed by, and the guilt of its destructive effects belong to, the evil human intellect."[32] This type of sorcerer then would seem to possess powers of mental projection equivalent to those of a witch, though seemingly lacking the capacity for physical metamorphosis.

The named category of thinkers seems restricted to the Western Cherokee, since it is not encountered in any known Eastern Cherokee texts. However, in the latter body of materials, another term is found that may be a functional equivalent to Oklahoma Cherokee thinkers. This term *uya i:gawé:ski gewa* is rendered by Mooney[33] as "imprecator" and can be literally translated as "evil, speaker of it, he."[34] My informant in 1959 confirmed the usage of this term as "bad talker," "bad conjurer," or "curser." This native term for "imprecator" apparently does not occur in Oklahoma, although the prefix *uya* or *u:yaga* was interpreted by one of the Kilpatricks's informants as "an evil earth-spirit."[35] I suspect that these two terms, *thinkers* and *imprecators* are functionally equivalent, though obviously differing etymologically, since Cherokee practitioners recognize a continuity between thinking, uttering, and singing *idi:gawé:sdi*;[36] the continuity emerges through a focusing of mental concentration believed to be essential to the effective performance of the ritual.

Knowledge of sorcery is generally acquired gradually, usually over the course of a lifetime. While perhaps not always the case, sorcerers tend to be men in contemporary Cherokee society and also in the time of Mooney's and Olbrechts's investigations. In the normal process a young man places himself under the tutelage of an accomplished medicine man (*dida:hnvw:sgi*, "curer of them, he"). The medicine man assesses the student's aptitude, motivation, and general character, often utilizing divinatory procedures. If the applicant is judged suitable, instruction proceeds gradually through a knowledge of medicinal plants, curing rituals, procedures, and techniques, including transmission of written *idi:gawé:sdi*. The most dangerous rituals, those intended to cause misfortune to others, are only imparted after the instructor is convinced that such knowledge will not be abused by the fledgling medicine man. Olbrechts describes a kind of "postgraduate" ordeal in which the supplicant repairs to a secluded place in the woods or mountains where he subsists on a decoction made from the inner bark of sweet birch (*Betale lenta* L.) and the root of Golden Alexander (*Zizia aurea* [L.]).[37] If he maintains this vigil for four days, he will become a gifted medicine man; if he extends the ordeal for a full seven days, he becomes a powerful wizard capable of flying through the air or of burrowing through the ground. This procedure is practically identical to that described previously for becoming a witch, except for the different plants used and the fact that the individual undergoing the latter ritual has been carefully selected and trained in the principles of Cherokee medicine and, presumably, will utilize his exceptional powers only for positive ends.

Other individuals may acquire a more limited knowledge of sorcery by inheriting or acquiring relevant *idi:gawé:sdi* and being instructed in their use by a consenting practitioner. However, such partial knowledge is considered as dangerous to possess, especially since sorcery, when ineffectively controlled, may be returned in harmful fashion to the sender.

Several general conclusions emerge from this brief survey of named Cherokee categories within the recognizable domain of sorcery and witchcraft. First, witches are not genetically endowed with mystical powers, although special rituals might be performed at birth to make the infant into a witch. Indi-

viduals also might undergo rituals later in life to enable them
to attain the powers of a witch. Second, witches are regarded
as essentially evil creatures who cause misfortune directly
through acts of will or through metamorphosis. Third, various
other medicomagical practitioners might acquire specific
knowledge of techniques to do harm to, or even kill, another
human being; however, such knowledge was thought of as
subject to cultural control and only invoked with just cause.
Fourth, some exceptional medicomagical practitioners could
acquire powers equivalent to those of witches, including the
capacity for metamorphosis, such that at this level the implicit
functional contrast between witches and sorcerers disappears,
except perhaps for motivations in exercising this mystical
power and the manner in which it was attained. It was also
suggested that Cherokee beliefs in witches is grounded in their
system of ethics and ideas about the nature of persons. It is
to this point that I return in concluding this essay.

Robert Thomas, in a brilliant unpublished paper on values
and world view, sees the core of the traditional value system
as the effort of the culturally conservative Cherokee "to maintain harmonious interpersonal relationships with his fellow
Cherokee by avoiding giving offense on the negative side, and
by giving of himself to his fellow Cherokee in regard to his
time and material goods on the positive side."[38] I have been
unable to discover a Cherokee term directly corresponding to
Thomas's postulation of the undoubted Cherokee value on
maintaining interpersonal harmony. However, Jack Kilpatrick
has pointed out to me the overriding Cherokee commitment
to a sense of justice in human relations.[39] This sense of justice,
supported by human warmth and good will, is embodied in
the Cherokee notion of *duyu:gh(o):dv́*, a term defying precise
translation, but connoting the adjectives "just," "right,"
"straight," "honest," "true," and "upright."[40] It is considered
a positive life force, and the Cherokees manifest an extreme
sensitivity to violations of *duyu:gh(o):dv́*, or to what they regard as injustice. Feuds and factionalism, which have been
endemic and transgenerational features of Cherokee history,

have their roots in perceived violations of this implicit sense of justice.

Underlying this ethical belief in *duyu:gh(o):dv́* is a classification of people into two diametrically opposed moral types. A person is either *u:da:nv:ti*, which refers to a man of "soul," "heart," or "feeling" and whose behavior can be summarized as being essentially "kind," or an individual is regarded as *u:ne:go:tso:dv́*, or unmitigatingly evil. It is important to emphasize that the contrast is not between "good," in the righteous sense, and "evil," but between "kind" and "evil." The classification is absolute, and a person does not shift categories according to the situation or over the course of a lifetime. A Cherokee may know a man for years before consigning him to one category or the other, but once made the classification is irrevocable. A kind man can commit errors, or in the Christian sense be guilty of sin, even to the extent of murder, but a man so classified possesses an essential humanity and can be forgiven. He shares an almost Durkheimian mechanical solidarity with his fellow Cherokee. If his breach of ethical conduct is so severe as to endanger the physical or moral well-being of the group, he willingly surrenders himself to that group and suffers the consequences of his actions. Cherokee history contains several examples of such martyrs.

In contrast, an individual who is regarded as *u:ne:go:tso:dv́* is viewed as a personification of human evil, one who operates unjustly from the "blackness" of his soul. Such an individual may be excluded from the human community and be written off as dead—and given the proper time and place, he will be. So-called political homicide is also not an infrequent phenomenon to anyone with even a casual acquaintance with Cherokee history.[41]

From this perspective of ethnopersonality theory, evil individuals, whether or not they possess the extraordinary powers attributed to witches, may be considered the moral equivalent of witches. It can be argued further that evil individuals and witches fall outside the realm of humanity. Witches must be regarded as counterfeit or pseudohuman beings since humanity is but one among many guises that they assume in their incessant metamorphoses and in their parasitic relationship to the Cherokee community.

NOTES

1. I wish to thank the American Philosophical Society for providing funds for the fieldwork on which this paper is based and the Division of Social Sciences of the University of Chicago for travel money that enabled me to present this paper. This paper was originally envisioned as part of a collaborative effort between Charles Holzinger and myself. I wish to credit him for stimulation during the early phases of preparation and I also want to acknowledge the criticism and encouragement of the following people: Carlos Dabezies, Charles Hudson, Paul Kutsche, William Sturtevant, and Albert Wahrhaftig.

2. John Haywood, *The Natural and Aboriginal History of Tennessee, up to the First Settlements Therein by the White People, in the Year 1768* (Nashville: George Wilson, 1823), pp. 267–268.

3. James Mooney, *Myths of the Cherokee*, Nineteenth Annual Report of the Bureau of American Ethnology, 1897–1898 (Washington, D.C., 1900), p. 138, citing Cephus Washburn, 1869.

4. James Mooney, *Sacred Formulas of the Cherokee*, Seventh Annual Report of the Bureau of American Ethnology (Washington, D.C., 1891).

5. Cf. Jack F. Kilpatrick and Anna G. Kilpatrick, *Run toward the Nightland: Magic of the Oklahoma Cherokees* (Dallas, Tex.: Southern Methodist University Press, 1967).

6. Jack F. Kilpatrick and Anna G. Kilpatrick, *Walk in Your Soul: Love Incantations of the Oklahoma Cherokees* (Dallas, Tex.: Southern Methodist University Press, 1965), pp. 4–8.

7. James Mooney and Frans M. Olbrechts, *The Swimmer Manuscript*, Smithsonian Institution, Bureau of American Ethnology Bulletin no. 99 (Washington, D.C., 1932).

8. Frank G. Speck and Leonard Broom, *Cherokee Dance and Drama* (Berkeley and Los Angeles: University of California Press, 1951); John Witthoft, *Green Corn Ceremonialism in the Eastern Woodlands*, Occasional Contributions from the Museum of Anthropology of the University of Michigan, no. 13 (Ann Arbor: University of Michigan Press, 1949); John Witthoft and Wendell S. Hadlock, "Cherokee-Iroquois Little People," *Journal of American Folklore* 59 (1946): 413–422.

9. Raymond D. Fogelson, "A Study of the Conjuror in Eastern Cherokee Society" (M.A. thesis, University of Pennsylvania, 1958); idem, "Change, Persistence, and Accommodation in Cherokee Medico-magical Beliefs," in *Symposium on Cherokee and Iroquois Culture*, ed. William N. Fenton and John Gulick, Smithsonian Institution, Bureau of American Ethnology Bulletin no. 180 (Washington D.C., 1961); idem, "The Cherokee Ballgame: A Study in Southeastern Indian Ethnology" (Ph.D. diss., University of Pennsylvania, 1962); idem, "The Cherokee Ballgame Cycle: An Ethnographer's View," *Ethnomusicology* 15 (1971): 327–333.

10. Jack F. Kilpatrick, *The Siqusnid' Dil'tidegi Collection*, Southern Methodist University, Bridewell Library (Dallas, Tex.: Bridewell Library, 1962) ; idem, "Folk Formulas of the Oklahoma Cherokees," *Journal of the Folklore Institute* 1 (1964) : 214–219; Jack F. Kilpatrick and Anna G. Kilpatrick, "Cherokee Burn Conjurations," *Journal Graduate Research Center* (S.M.U.) 33 (1964) : 17–21; idem, "A Cherokee Conjuration to Cure a Horse," *Southern Folklore Quarterly* 28 (1964) : 216–218; idem, "The Foundation of Life: The Cherokee National Ritual," *American Anthropologist* 66 (1964) : 1386–1389.

11. Jack F. Kilpatrick and Anna G. Kilpatrick, "Notebook of a Cherokee Shaman," *Smithsonian Contributions to Anthropology* 2 (1970) : 83–125.

12. Clyde Kluckhohn, *Navaho Witchcraft* (Boston: Beacon Press, 1944) .

13. E. E. Evans-Pritchard, *Witchcraft, Oracles, and Magic among the Azande* (Oxford: Clarendon Press, 1937) .

14. John F. Middleton and Edward Winter, eds., *Witchcraft and Sorcery in East Africa* (London: Routledge and Kegan Paul, 1963) .

15. Victor W. Turner, "Witchcraft and Sorcery: Taxonomy versus Dynamics," *Africa* 34 (1964) : 319–324.

16. Mary Douglas, ed., *Witchcraft Confessions and Accusations*, Association of Social Anthropologists Monograph 9 (London: Tavistock Publications, 1970) .

17. Deward Walker, ed., *Systems of North American Witchcraft and Sorcery*. Anthropological Monographs of the University of Idaho no. 1 (Moscow: University of Idaho, 1970) .

18. Mooney and Olbrechts, *Swimmer Manuscript*, p. 29.

19. Ibid., p. 29.

20. Kilpatrick and Kilpatrick, *Walk in Your Soul*, p. 9.

21. Mooney and Olbrechts, *Swimmer Manuscript*, p. 88.

22. Ibid., p. 130.

23. Charles H. Holzinger, unpublished field notes, 1957.

24. Mooney and Olbrechts, *Swimmer Manuscript*, p. 130.

25. Ibid., p. 131.

26. Ibid., p. 30.

27. The English term *witch* has been almost universally adopted among North American Indian groups and in other areas where there has been significant Anglo-American influence. However I have yet to encounter any native group that has adopted the English term *sorcerer,* and the term seems of infrequent usage in popular parlance in the English-speaking world.

28. Kilpatrick and Kilpatrick, *Walk in Your Soul*, p. 9.

29. Mooney and Olbrechts, *Swimmer Manuscript*, p. 87.

30. Kilpatrick and Kilpatrick, "Notebook of a Cherokee Shaman," p. 97.

31. Kilpatrick and Kilpatrick, *Run toward the Nightland*, p. 170.

32. Kilpatrick and Kilpatrick, "Notebook of a Cherokee Shaman," p. 97.

33. James Mooney, *Sacred Formulas of the Cherokee*, p. 384.

34. Cf. Mooney and Olbrechts, *Swimmer Manuscript*, p. 256; Kilpatrick and Kilpatrick, "Notebook of a Cherokee Shaman," p. 100.

35. Kilpatrick and Kilpatrick, "Notebook of a Cherokee Shaman," p. 100.

36. Cf. Marcia Herndon, "The Cherokee Ballgame Cycle: An Ethnomusicologist's View," *Ethnomusicology* 15 (1971) : 349–350.

37. Mooney and Olbrechts, *Swimmer Manuscript*, p. 102.

38. Robert K. Thomas, "Cherokee Values and World View," MS, 1958, p. 1.

39. Jack F. Kilpatrick, personal communication, 30 July 1966.

40. Jack F. Kilpatrick and Anna G. Kilpatrick, *The Shadow of Sequoyah: Social Documents of the Cherokees, 1862–1964,* University of Oklahoma, Civilization of the American Indian Series no. 81, (Norman: University of Oklahoma Press, 1965) , p. 9.

41. The well-known political assassinations of Elias Boudinot, Major Ridge, and John Ridge in the Indian Territory in 1839, and the long trail of blood ensuing from these events, serve as cases in point.

SOURCES CITED

Douglas, Mary, ed. *Witchcraft Confessions and Accusations.* Association of Social Anthropologists Monograph 9. London: Tavistock Publications, 1970.

Evans-Pritchard, E. E. *Witchcraft, Oracles, and Magic among the Azande.* Oxford: Clarendon Press, 1937.

Fogelson, Raymond D. "Change, Persistence, and Accommodation in Cherokee Medico-Magical Beliefs." In *Symposium on Cherokee and Iroquois Culture,* edited by W. N. Fenton and John Gulick, pp. 215–225. Smithsonian Institution. Bureau of American Ethnology Bulletin no. 180. Washington, D.C., 1961.

———. "The Cherokee Ballgame: A Study in Southeastern Indian Ethnology." Ph.D. dissertation, University of Pennsylvania, 1962.

———. "The Cherokee Ballgame Cycle: An Ethnographer's View." *Ethnomusicology* 15 (1971) : 327–338.

———. "A Study of the Conjuror in Eastern Cherokee Society." M.A. thesis, University of Pennsylvania, 1958.

Haywood, John. *The Natural and Aboriginal History of Tennessee, up to the First Settlements Therein by the White People, in the Year 1768.* Nashville, 1823.

Herndon, Marcia. "The Cherokee Ballgame Cycle: An Ethnomusicologist's View." *Ethnomusicology* 15 (1971) : 339–352.

Holzinger, Charles H. Unpublished field notes. 1957.

Kilpatrick, Jack F. "Folk Formulas of the Oklahoma Cherokees." *Journal Folklore Institute* 1 (1964) : 214–219.

———. Personal communication. 30 July 1966.

———. *The Siqusnid' Dil'tidegi Collection.* Southern Methodist University. Bridewell Library. Dallas, Tex.: Bridewell Library, 1962.

———, and Kilpatrick, Anna G. "Cherokee Burn Conjurations." *Journal Graduate Research Center* (Southern Methodist University) 33 (1964) : 17–21.

———. "A Cherokee Conjuration to Cure a Horse." *Southern Folklore Quarterly* 28 (1964) : 216–218.

———. "The Foundation of Life: The Cherokee National Ritual." *American Anthropologist* 66 (1964) : 1386–1389.

———. "Notebook of a Cherokee Shaman." *Smithsonian Contributions to Anthropology* 2 (1970) : 83–125.

———. *Run toward the Nightland: Magic of the Oklahoma Cherokees.* Dallas, Tex.: Southern Methodist University Press, 1967.

———. *The Shadow of Sequoyah: Social Documents of the Cherokees, 1862– 1964.* University of Oklahoma Civilization of the American Indian Series no. 81. Norman: University of Oklahoma Press, 1965.

———. *Walk in Your Soul: Love Incantations of the Oklahoma Cherokees.* Dallas, Tex.: Southern Methodist University Press, 1965.

Kluckhohn, Clyde. *Navaho Witchcraft.* Boston: Beacon Press, 1944.

Middleton, John F., and Winter, Edward, eds. *Witchcraft and Sorcery in East Africa.* London: Routledge and Kegan Paul, 1963.

Mooney, James. *Myths of the Cherokee.* Smithsonian Institution. Nineteenth Annual Report of the Bureau of American Ethnology, 1897–1898. Washington, D.C., 1900.

———. *Sacred Formulas of the Cherokee.* Smithsonian Institution. Seventh Annual Report of the Bureau of American Ethnology. Washington, D.C., 1891.

———, and Olbrechts, Frans M. *The Swimmer Manuscript.* Smithsonian Institution. Bureau of American Ethnology Bulletin no. 99. Washington, D.C., 1932.

Speck, Frank G., and Broom, Leonard. *Cherokee Dance and Drama.* Berkeley and Los Angeles: University of California Press, 1951.

Thomas, Robert K. "Cherokee Values and World View." MS. 1958.

Turner, Victor W. "Witchcraft and Sorcery: Taxonomy versus Dynamics." *Africa* 34 (1964): 319–324.

Walker, Deward, ed. *Systems of North American Witchcraft and Sorcery.* Anthropological Monographs of the University of Idaho no. 1. Moscow: University of Idaho, 1970.

Witthoft, John. *Green Corn Ceremonialism in the Eastern Woodlands.* University of Michigan. Museum of Anthropology, no. 13. Ann Arbor: University of Michigan Press, 1949.

———, and Hadlock, Wendell S. "Cherokee-Iroquois Little People." *Journal of American Folklore* 59 (1946): 413–422.

Institution Building among Oklahoma's Traditional Cherokees

Albert L. Wahrhaftig

The Cherokee Indians are known as a "civilized tribe." They were called that by Europeans who were impressed by Cherokee accomplishments, for in barely a century the Cherokees established and maintained a national school system, a bicameral legislature, a press and newspaper, a system of local and supreme courts, a national police force—in short, the entire institutional complex characteristic of a European nation. The Cherokee rise to recognizable nationhood, as documented by Europeans and Americans, was rapid and impressive.

As early as 1796 the letters of Benjamin Hawkins chronicled Cherokee progress in the material arts of agriculture, animal husbandry, spinning, weaving, and homemaking.[1] By 1817 the tribe had established a national bicameral legislature. In 1821 Sequoyah's invention of a Cherokee syllabary was complete. A Cherokee could learn to read and write his own language in a matter of days, and those who did not do so were few. A National Superior Court was instituted in 1822, and in 1827 the Cherokees adopted both a written constitution and sanctioned the establishment of a national press. While a lesser nation might have been shattered by the forced removal from their homelands over the Trail of Tears which followed the signing of the Treaty of New Echota in 1835, the Cherokees not only survived but quickly reestablished their institutions.

By 1840 the Cherokee National Council was in session at the new capitol in Tahlequah. Less than five years after arriving in a new wilderness, the Cherokees were adding to their national apparatus. Most notably, a national system of public schools was created in 1841, and funds for male and female seminaries (high schools) were appropriated in 1846.

How did such institutions come into being? Although Cherokee developments are described at length in a number of readily available histories of the tribe, this basic question of social process remains unanswered. Present-day observations provide some insight into these historic social processes. Based on case histories collected during my anthropological fieldwork in Oklahoma, I am prepared to argue that traditional, conservative, localized communities of Indians—precisely the people Oklahomans call "fullbloods"—are the primary source of institutional innovation within the Cherokee tribe.

My thesis runs against the grain of at least two presently held interpretations of Cherokee dynamics. At one extreme there is the view of scholars who assert that Cherokee national development came about through the efforts of a centrally located, highly educated elite of "mixed bloods." This explanation is frequently wedded to a naive racism, as in the case of Morris Wardell who wrote:

> Traders, soldiers, and treaty-makers came among the Cherokees to trade, compel and negotiate. Some of these visitors married Indian women and lived in the Indian villages the remainder of their days. Children born to such unions preferred the open and free life and here grew to manhood and womanhood, never going to the white settlements. This mixture of blood helped to produce the strategy and cleverness which made formidable diplomats of many of the Indian leaders.[2]

Interpretation in this tradition finds a more recent representative in Grace Steele Woodward who asserts that

> many of the full bloods in eastern Oklahoma today are lagging woefully behind the mixed-bloods, economically,

socially, and morally. They supplement their small income from farms and subsidies from the government with wage work or seasonal jobs in nearby towns or on farms belonging to white men. . . . Paid fair wages, this type of worker usually spends his money as quickly as he makes it on whisky, and on cars, washing machines, and other items that, uncared for, soon fall into necessitous disuse.[3]

At the other extreme, there is the modern Oklahoma ethos in which the current Indian affairs establishment and those who support it are conceived of as a "progressive element," which rightly directs programs to benefit "backward fullbloods in the hills."[4]

My own suggestion is simply that the flow of innovation is from the bottom up, as it were, and not from the top down. In the cases I am about to relate, elderly and traditional men "from the hills" called the shots. Often the very person they called forth as their spokesman was at the same time related to by whites as a "leader," that is, as a man very much oriented to Euro-American society and as a man trying to "bring his people forward into the twentieth century." Indeed, I suspect that the autonomous Cherokee Nation, which lasted until it was dissolved by whites in 1907, may have been built by men who received credit from whites for accomplishments demanded of them by their traditional elders.

In this study I am speaking primarily about how contemporary Oklahoma Cherokees get things done and not about the social system that contains them. Still, these are inseparable, and I must explain by way of background that today's Cherokees are powerless and extremely poor. As Angie Debo's meticulously documented work demonstrates, "the white man's guardianship," especially in a period that extended from the 1880s into the 1920s, stripped the tribe of its autonomous nationhood, its land, and its resources.[5] As a result there is now a startling disparity between Cherokee and white well-being in eastern Oklahoma. As an index, Cherokee per capita income is less than one-half that of neighboring whites who are themselves classified as a "poverty population."

WHITE AND CHEROKEE PER CAPITA INCOME, OKLAHOMA, 1963

County	*White per capita income*	*Cherokee per capita income*	*Cherokee income as percent of white*
Adair	$1,090	$465	43%
Cherokee	1,270	590	47
Delaware	1,320	555	42
Sequoyah	1,090	445	41

SOURCE: Albert L. Wahrhaftig, *Social and Economic Characteristics of the Tribal Cherokee Population of Eastern Oklahoma*, Anthropological Studies no. 5 (Washington, D.C.: American Anthropological Association, 1970), p. 47, table 5.4.

Now, humiliatingly, the Cherokees see their tribal affairs directed by a local establishment made up of members of the Bureau of Indian Affairs, the Chamber of Commerce, other interested state and federal bureaucracies, and by the Cherokee tribal government. As an ex-member of the Cherokee tribal government told a Senate subcommittee:

> The Cherokees have had imposed upon them a federally appointed chief. He is appointed by the President of the United States upon the recommendation of the Secretary of the Interior. The Cherokees have nothing to say about it.
>
> In 1948, when Mr. Bartley Milam was chief, an election was called for the purpose of selecting a representative from each of the former nine Cherokee districts to select lawyers to represent the Cherokees in their claims against the U.S. Government. Mr. Milam died shortly after this, and the present chief has perpetuated this committee, calling it the Cherokee Executive Committee. There has never been another election, and this committee is now made up of the chief's appointees.[6]

The chief's appointees are for the most part local businessmen who can claim a "little bit of Indian blood," but whose families have lived away from traditional Cherokee communities and among whites for generations.[7] Murray Wax sums up the situation by calling the Cherokees "an administered people" whose economy is "perilously close to bare existence" and for whom such white service bureaucracies as the welfare department "represent an awful and irresponsible power."[8] Under these circumstances it is amazing that Cherokees have been able to retain any shred of control over the initiation of institutions within their own communities. Let me now offer an example of institutional flux within contemporary Cherokee communities.

When first seen by Europeans in their ancestral territory in the Southeast, Cherokees lived in "towns," that is, in aggregates of households with a central ceremonial meeting place, the whole distributed along a waterway or in a hollow. The same settlement pattern is found in Oklahoma today. In southern Adair County, Oklahoma, there is an area where two such Cherokee communities overlap. One is centered around Echota Cherokee Indian Baptist Church. The other consists of members of the Four Mothers Society[9] who worship at a non-Christian dance ground near the home of their chief, Jim Wolfe. Members of each of these communities feel that they practice the true Cherokee way and that their Cherokee neighbors of different ritual persuasion "don't know what's right." However, in these circumstances, Cherokees simply refrain from interfering in the affairs of others. In these particular communities there is a higher than average percentage, in fact a majority, of people who speak Cherokee and do not understand English. There is also, especially among the Baptists at Echota, a faction of people who actively wish to emulate white men. In 1964 this faction collaborated with a white missionary who wanted to modernize the church by encouraging the congregation to abandon "backward" practices such as singing, preaching, and reading the Bible in Cherokee. As a result the church was soon dominated by a very young and white-oriented Cherokee pastor and his followers, under whose direction youngsters in Sunday school were taught scripture exclusively in English from English language tracts. As many Cherokees learn to read Sequoyah syllables in Baptist

Sunday School, and as the acquisition of literacy in Cherokee is itself thought of as a sacred and highly desirable act, this was a change of enormous consequence.

The response was that a number of the older men from the Echota Baptist congregation (the opinion makers of the community) approached their non-Christian neighbors, the members of the Four Mothers Society. Speaking of what had happened to their church, they said, "The way it is, we might just as well send our children to the white man's church down the road." Then they waited a few weeks for word to get around.

Nothing changed at Echota Church, and so the old men came back and sat again with the men of the Four Mothers Society. They said it wasn't any use to let their children become white men, but then, they couldn't see their way towards joining the Four Mothers Society for worship, for theirs was the Christian way. Why not, they decided, join forces to build a Sunday school where Christian and non-Christian together could teach their children to read and write Cherokee. That much they could agree on, and each could continue to worship where and as they chose. It took some weeks of discussion for this idea to emerge, but eventually things got to the point of a definite understanding. A piece of land was set aside. A stand of trees was reserved for timber. A mason volunteered his skills. There was thinking going on about how to raise money for other materials. A new institution was being built.

I say a new institution first because this school, as it was planned, would not have coincided with the social boundaries of either of the preexisting communities. It would have been shared by interested members of both. More significantly, in this new institution formal instruction in Cherokee literacy would have been removed from a specifically sacred context for the first time in this century.

There were more subtle aspects to the situation. When Cherokees heartily disapprove of the behavior of their fellows, and when they wish to be coercive, they *withdraw*. "Withdrawal," of course, is our word for what is, for Cherokees, a nasty falling-out among relatives (since communities are knit by kinship) and, what is worse, it threatens to lead to precisely the kind of situation in which people conjure one another. As is often the case with people who live in close and permanent interdependence, Cherokees go to extremes to avoid giving offense to others. Lacking any sanctioned means of openly displaying hostility, Cherokees discharge any accumulated hard feelings by withdrawal and as a final resort by approaching Indian "doctors" and hiring them to cast evil spells upon their enemies. In this instance, the old men of Echota were playing "heads I win, tails you lose." Their proposal to build a new institution was a threat of withdrawal, and therefore also an ultimatum to an existing institution. They carried their point. As soon as it was legally possible, the congregation replaced the young white-emulating preacher with a seasoned pastor known far and wide as a master of traditional Cherokee ways. The opinion makers again occupied their pews, and what should we say of the "new institution?" That it never got off the ground? Or that it had already served its purpose?

It would be easy to read this as an example of rigid conservatism, of a community forcing reformers to toe the line. Rather, I believe it illustrates a process generally true of Cherokees. Cherokees innovate when it is necessary to do so in order to keep their way of life intact. Not unchanged, but intact. We see here a contemporary expression of an old pattern. After all, Sequoyah *could* have learned to read and write English. Instead, seeing the necessity of written preservation of knowledge and the utility of written communications, he invented a Cherokee writing system. Active and inquisitive to the end of his long years, he still had not found it worth his while to learn to speak English.

From the Cherokee point of view, what is essential in their institutions is the communication of the stuff of what it is to be Cherokee. The Cherokees, too, believe themselves civilized, and what is a civilized person if not one who through literacy has access to great truth preserved in writing? A separate literacy school, perhaps the germ of a system of secular education, is clearly an institutional innovation. But what of a church brought through crisis to an awareness of the importance of the tradition and learning conveyed within its rituals? Is this not an institution transformed?

I do not wish to leave the impression that all Cherokee innovations succeed negatively. Far from it. Indeed, as a second generality I would assert that wherever Cherokees find elbowroom to do so, they attempt to enrich life by adding educational, economic, charitable, and recreational activities to the one remaining institution which integrates their local communities—the neighborhood Indian church or dance ground. (Being a poor and an exploited people, they do not often find much elbowroom, however.) For instance, in northern Adair County, there are two more interpenetrating traditional Cherokee communities. One is clustered about the Illinois River Cherokee Indian Baptist Church, and the other consists of the membership of the Seven Clans Society which meets on a dance ground near Chewey. The dream of this population, for so long as I have known them, has been of a common and autonomous economic base: a co-op store, a local credit union, a tractor to share, a mechanical shop where young graduates of Haskell might work, and a merger of houses of worship with a new Baptist church standing alongside a refurbished dance ground. All of this takes money, of course. In an effort to raise some money, in the spring of 1967 two new structures were built on the ceremonial dance ground of the Seven Clans Society—an elevated bandstand and a refreshment shack. Over the following spring and summer weekends a band composed of local Cherokees played country swing music, attracting Cherokees, neighboring whites, and, as word spread, tourists weekending along the Illinois River. As time passed, local rock groups, both Indian and white, claimed a share of the program, and later the bandstand became a place for local Indian and white fiddlers to parade their style. There were times when the whole mélange stayed into the night for a traditional Cherokee "stomp dance." Meanwhile the community profited from a lively sale of soft drinks and hamburgers. The inventiveness of this arrangement is more apparent if one bears in mind that these communities are located in the Bible Belt, that the sobriety of Cherokee Baptists equals that of their white counterparts and that we are talking about honky-tonk musicians playing on sacred premises, or, in more formal terms, of a restructuring of the community such that former outcasts now have created for themselves central and useful roles. In this instance, the institutional structure of a Cherokee community was expanded to include new activities, new internal relationships, a new source of income, and a new complex of relationships with white neighbors.

A more dramatic case of institution building can be described. The "core" of the Oklahoma Cherokee tribe consists of some fifty small communities spread over six counties of eastern Oklahoma where Cherokees are isolated both by their own desire to withdraw from white men and by intense, though usually covert, racism on the part of local whites. Four generations of such isolation have left the Cherokees a people unsophisticated in the ways of the general society, and although this is generally an economically deprived area, the gulf in wealth and sophistication is increasing rapidly. The Cherokees resent what is happening to them. They believe that the remnants of their land are being stolen, that the welfare system is operated as a mechanism to divest them of their real property, that they are given prejudicial treatment in courts of law, that public schools abuse their children, and that their own tribal government consists of white men who claim to be Indian in order to secure fat salaries and to get closer to Cherokee funds. In 1965 this diffuse resentment crystallized—as it has in many Indian communities all over the country—on the issue of hunting and fishing. With the blessings of their elders, the men of two Cherokee communities, somehow discovering that they felt the same about this grievance, formed a secret organization with the intent of going hunting all together and daring the white man to make an issue of it. Within months this community-based organization expanded in three dimensions. Its territory and organizational complexity were augmented as enthusiasm spread and need arose, until it had become a complex institution with representation by "district" and by community. From one meeting to the next, the scope of issues presented to it by Cherokees in successive communities snowballed. People wanted to deal with land losses, with welfare rights, with acquisition of literacy in Cherokee, with grievances against public schools, with treaty rights, with inadequacies in tribal enrollment determinations, and, always first and foremost, with Cherokee rights to hunt and fish. The ties of this organization into the institutional framework outside the Cherokee community proliferated. Through it, in the course of one year, Cherokees sought aid and advice from the Community Relations Service (then of the Department of Commerce), from the Office of Economic Opportunity, from anthropologists, from foundations, and from private lawyers. The organization entered the courts to "back up" (as the Cherokees phrased it) one young Cherokee charged with hunting out of season, and when it appeared that this case might be heard eventually by the United States Supreme Court, interest in the organization and faith that the Cherokees might after all receive justice from the American legal system was unbounded. At this point there was a dramatic increase in the number of Cherokee communities participating through representatives.

Within months a complex, multipurpose, occasionally underground and secret, tribe-wide institution emerged.[10] Ponderously named the Five County Northeastern Oklahoma Cherokee Organization (later the Original Cherokee Community Organization), its structure and procedures reflected the power and innovative impetus of constituent Cherokee communities. Policies were discussed at meetings open to all speakers of the Cherokee language and decisions were reached by consensus. All letters and telegrams addressed to the chairman and secretary of the organization were read aloud at these meetings. Meetings were rotated from one county to the next and within counties from one to another host community in an effort to exclude no Cherokee from direct participation. A Declaration of the Five County Cherokees, adopted in July 1966, commenced by stating

We, the Five County Cherokees, are one people.
We stand united in the sight of God, our Creator.
We are joined by love and concern for each other and for all men.

These are our purposes:
We offer ourselves as the voice of the Cherokee people. For many years our people have not spoken and have not been heard. We Cherokees have always known that a free people speak, both, with the voice of the whole people, and with the voice of each individual person. Among Cherokees, each man has his own way of thinking. We have always had many different organizations, each doing important things. We do not speak as a people until we can speak for every single Cherokee and every single organization. We leave each man and each organization among us free to do their proper job without hindrance or interference. When one Cherokee raises his voice, all Cherokees listen. Since the beginning of time, that has been the Cherokee way. Now we gather as brothers and sisters. We bring with us the belief and the opinions of each of our faiths and organizations. This is how we must speak out as one people. This way we will be listened to.[11]

Whenever relationships were established with organizations of the general society, the American Civil Liberties Union, for example, their representatives were urged—even pressured—to come and confront the Cherokee population directly. The many tasks that the organization attempted were entrusted to committees structured so that each county in which Cherokees live could be represented and so that each county could have its own subcommittee with representation by community.

Cherokee life was dramatically enriched by activities directed by committees of the Five County Cherokees. They inaugurated a newspaper in Sequoyah's Cherokee syllabary addressed to the concerns of local Cherokee communities (it is still being published) and a Cherokee language radio program filled with announcements of community meetings, gospel sings, and pie suppers. They began to compile their own archive of documents relating to continuing fraudulent sales of Cherokee lands, and eventually, pleading the need for legal education on a community level, they secured a grant from the Field Foundation which enabled them to hire their own lawyer. Their first instructions to him were to present himself in each Cherokee community to see what the people of each expected of him.

The Five County Cherokees never was an organization, though I have used that word, but rather it was a forum through which spokesmen of autonomous local communities could state their concerns and establish consensus among all whom they recognized as Cherokees, and it was also a fluid assemblage of committees designed to coordinate tasks specified by local communities. A new superstructure was rapidly emerging from the concerns of each man's community.

For one heady and magical year, the Cherokees were doing things again, and the resultant feelings of accomplishment fueled the ambitions of local communities and removed the ceiling from long suppressed aspirations. It was precisely during this period that the people of Chewey reconciled sober Baptists, honky-tonk fiddlers, and rock-playing youth and expanded the institutional structure of their community to accommodate the energies of these disparate groups.

If the rapid pace at which these innovations occurred still demands explanation, it is because the account has to this point been phrased in secular terms although the Cherokees are a people who live under prophecy. At the turn of this century when intruding white men were surveying the Cherokees' commonly held land into individual allotments, listing people in roll books, and preparing to "take the Cherokees' laws away" (as older Cherokees say, "when the State come in") in an act of despair the most powerful Indian doctors of the tribe collaborated to divine the future of the people. The details of these prophecies is an esoteric body of knowledge known to a few native specialists, but I never met a Cherokee who had not internalized those predictions in broad outline. It was seen that the people, for having strayed from their appointed path, were destined to suffer adversity. What they had would be taken from them. More tragically, sons and daughters would shun their fathers and mothers, thus reducing the Cherokees in number to but a tiny core of their population. But that core would be a nucleus of true and steadfast people and when the grinding down had run its course, then from the stock who had retained their faith in Cherokee ways would the nation be restored. In this context, the theft and bigotry and oppression that surround the modern Cherokee becomes intelligible. In this context also, any achievement— the first gatherings of people resolved to come to grips with a problem such as hunting and fishing, in this instance—can be interpreted as a sign that the times have turned. Even the suspicion that this might be the case can fire a people with messianic energy. The oldest men among the Five County Cherokees said it was "like in Cherokee Nation days," and rather than view their assessment as nostalgia, I think it was realistically accurate. They perhaps felt again the emotive quality of life in the old Cherokee Nation: an existence that is vivid, decisive, exciting. In addition, the Five County Cherokees, like the Cherokee Nation, was a social innovation, a new arrangement of people and a new configuration of custom over the preexisting technological and economic base. Finally, both involved the accomplishment of a new heterogeneity: the reconciliation of youth schooled in foreign ways with domestic masters of tradition.

It grieves me to report that the celebrated hunting rights case[12] was buried in legal procrastination and that the Cherokees became skeptical of their new organization. The fact that the first chairman was a charismatic figure with a golden tongue but also a larcenous disposition hastened disenchantment, but on the whole, this new Cherokee institution was simply dismembered by the Cherokees' own tribal government.[13] The Cherokee government and the Bureau of Indian Affairs felt their power was being subverted by the rapidly growing new organization. They began competing for adherents by duplicating every service initiated by the Five County Cherokees and by relating directly to individual Cherokee communities for the first time. Both the Cherokee government and the Bureau of Indian Affairs hired their first

Cherokee-speaking community workers. Utilizing financial advantages to the utmost and working through a new system of community representatives, they seeded housing projects in each Cherokee community until Cherokees were lured back into the fold. The establishment preserved its power intact, but at the price of finally granting official recognition to the existence of the very communities we have been talking about.

Cherokee institutional innovation occurs as novel solutions to the problem of maintaining the basic and definitive relationships which sustain the people in each settlement throughout the tribe. When threatening events interfere with these relationships and bring them into awareness, the Cherokees will experiment with anything which offers the promise of protecting and reinforcing that valued portion of their life. At Echota interference with the transmission of traditional literacy to the young nearly precipitated a new form of schools. At Chewey on the Illinois River a body of people created from homely materials institutions which bridge their ritual and ethnic differences. And from efforts to cope with disruption of one of their most meaningful endeavors, the right of the Cherokees to harvest the game left to them by their Apportioner, sprang the most comprehensive and impressive of modern Cherokee institutions. These institutions grew from the roots of Cherokee community life. The basic nature of the problems that prompted them gave them a direction and a meaning that no program proposed by outsiders could ever have. Thinking Cherokees are aware of this.

In 1968 the chairman of the Five County Cherokees watched as his membership was seduced away, but he said to me,

Watch what is going to happen. I know how these peoples are. They don't have a hand in how this thing is being done, and it won't suit them. Either that white man program will go wrong, and they won't get that house they been promised, and they will get mad, or they will get that house they have been promised, and it won't satisfy them. Maybe it won't be built good and they won't like it, and they will get mad. In two or three years they will all be back, and we will be looking for a new way.

NOTES

1. Benjamin Hawkins, *Letters of Benjamin Hawkins, 1796–1800*, Collections of the Georgia Historical Society, vol. 9 (Savannah, 1916.)

2. Morris Wardell, *A Political History of the Cherokee Nation* (Norman: University of Oklahoma Press, 1938) , p. iv.

3. Grace Steele Woodward, *The Cherokees* (Norman: University of Oklahoma Press, 1963) , p. 6.

4. Albert L. Wahrhaftig, "Renaissance and Repression: The Oklahoma Cherokee," *Trans-action*, February 1969, pp. 42–48.

5. Angie Debo, *And Still the Waters Run* (Princeton, N.J.: Princeton University Press, 1940.)

6. U.S., Congress, Senate, Special Subcommittee on Indian Education of the Committee on Labor and Public Welfare, *Hearings on the Study of the Education of Indian Children*, pt. 2, Twin Oaks, Okla., 90th Cong., 2d session, 1968, p. 546.

7. Peter Collier, "The Theft of a Nation: Apologies to the Cherokees," *Ramparts* 9 (1970) : 35–45. The first elections for principal chief since Oklahoma statehood were held in the summer of 1971. The incumbent chief was elected. All other tribal executive offices continue to be appointive.

8. Murray Wax, *Indian Americans: Unity and Diversity* (New York: Prentice-Hall, 1971) , pp. 103–104.

9. For the first history of this movement, see Robert W. Buchanan, "Patterns of Organization and Leadership among Contemporary Oklahoma Cherokees" (Ph.D. diss., University of Kansas, 1972) .

10. Robert K. Thomas, "The Redbird Smith Movement" in *Symposium on Cherokee and Iroquois Culture*, eds. William N. Fenton and John Gulick, Smithsonian Institution, Bureau of American Ethnology Bulletin no. 180 (Washington, D.C., 1961) , pp. 161–166. When the Cherokees removed to Oklahoma, the pre-Christian religion went underground, reappearing during the resistance to Oklahoma statehood. The Four Mothers Society arose among the Creek Indians of this period and was imported into the Cherokee Nation during the Redbird Smith Movement. The Four Mothers Society, the Seven Clans Society, and the Nighthawk Keetoowah Society (all of somewhat similar origin) have active traditional ceremonial grounds in eastern Oklahoma.

11. Five County Northeastern Oklahoma Cherokee Organization. "Declaration," MS in possession of the author.

12. For an account of this case, see Stan Steiner, *The New Indians* (New York: Harper and Row, 1968) , chap. 1.

13. Peter Collier describes the termination of a successful "hospital committee" which served as a liaison between the Cherokees and the U.S. Department of Public Health's Indian hospital in Tahlequah. Said the hospital's staff social worker, "I later found out that Keeler [principal chief of the Cherokee tribe] felt his authority had been challenged by this hospital committee. The director of the hospital admitted to me that Keeler had ordered them not to meet with the committee anymore. . . . He also made his feelings known to higher-ups in the public health department." Collier, "Theft of a Nation," p. 42.

SOURCES CITED

Buchanan, Robert W. "Patterns of Organization and Leadership among Contemporary Oklahoma Cherokees." Ph.D. diss., University of Kansas, 1972.

Collier, Peter. "The Theft of a Nation: Apologies to the Cherokees." *Ramparts* 9 (1970): 35–45.

Debo, Angie. *And Still the Waters Run*. Princeton, N.J.: Princeton University Press, 1940.

Five County Northeastern Oklahoma Cherokee Organization. "Declaration." MS.

Hawkins, Benjamin. *Letters of Benjamin Hawkins, 1796–1800*. Collections of the Georgia Historical Society, vol. 9. Savannah, 1916.

Steiner, Stan. *The New Indians*. New York: Harper and Row, 1968.

Thomas, Robert K. "The Redbird Smith Movement." In *Symposium on Cherokee and Iroquois Culture*, edited by William N. Fenton and John Gulick, pp. 161–166. Smithsonian Institution, Bureau of American Ethnology Bulletin no. 180. Washington, D.C., 1961.

U.S., Congress, Senate, Special Subcommittee on Indian Education of the Committee on Labor and Public Welfare. Hearings on the Study of the Education of Indian Children, pt. 2, Twin Oaks, Okla., 90th Congress, 2d session. Washington, D.C.: U.S. Government Printing Office, 1968.

Wahrhaftig, Albert L., and Thomas, Robert K. "Renaissance and Repression: The Oklahoma Cherokee." *Trans-action* 6 (1969): 42–48.

Wardell, Morris. *A Political History of the Cherokee Nation*. Norman: University of Oklahoma Press, 1938.

Wax, Murray. *Indian Americans: Unity and Diversity*. New York: Prentice-Hall, 1971.

Woodward, Grace Steele. *The Cherokees*. Norman: University of Oklahoma, 1963.

Indians and Blacks
in White America

Charles Crowe

During the colonial period of American history the aggressive confrontation of English imperialists with red and black men not only shaped American nationalism but also created the "white" man, the "Indian," and the "Negro." Although racial prejudices certainly existed in Elizabethan times, the Englishman regarded other factors as more fundamental than skin color. The imperial experience made "whiteness" the primary category of self-perception for Europeans and compelled the victims to consider their "blackness" and "redness." Before the catastrophic contacts with Europeans the native peoples of North America lacked a sense of common interest as well as collective names for themselves. Cherokees and Narragansetts did not and could not call themselves Indians, and similarly Ashantis and Ibos lacked any knowledge of either Africa or Negritude. "Discovery," defeat, and ultimate condemnation to plantations and reservations by Europeans gave to vastly different peoples the enduring names of Indian and Negro. Jean-Paul Sartre had something like this process in mind when he observed in a discussion of the Nazi era that "the anti-Semite creates the Jew" and in a prefatory analysis of imperialism for Frantz Fanon's celebrated book that "the settler manufactures the native."[1]

Sartre's observations do not, of course, reveal the whole truth. History cannot be reduced entirely to the plane of oppressors and their victims, and human creativity often transcends the most tyrannical circumstances. Black people, acting from desperately felt needs, combined what they could use

from the house of bondage with African remnants to establish a new Afro-American culture. Among the many creative
responses of the natives of America was the case of the Plains
Indians who made the white man's horse the central feature
in dynamic new life patterns. Although Europeans created
the Negroes and Indians they knew, conventional white chronicles fail to mention many of the most important facts about
these peoples. The victims have a separate history which is
an essential part of the contemporary struggle to define the
future. In certain respects the red man's true history even
predated the arrival of the Europeans, found expression during
the seventeenth and eighteenth centuries as the Iroquois,
Creek, and Cherokee confederacies, and continues in the
present with native American movements. Still, these developments happened contrary to or apart from the will of the
conquerors.[2]

When the Revolution established American nationality during the 1770s, the new citizen recognized himself first and foremost as a white man. Long before independence had become
an American dream, color was the dominant badge of status
in a society strongly oriented toward white supremacy. (This
powerful sense of whiteness even made the status of some
Europeans suspect. Benjamin Franklin described Germans as
"swarthy," fretted over the "very small" number of whites in
the world, and admitted only Englishmen and "Saxons" to the
racial elite.) The "whiteness" which emerged from the conquest and exploitation of red and black men symbolized a
conviction of superiority over "lesser breeds" around the world
as well as dominion over the North American continent and
its "inferior peoples."[3]

The general point can be extended and illustrated in a brief
discussion of the Chinese, a people virtually unknown to
Americans during the colonial and early national eras. George
Washington, who knew that the Chinese were "droll in shape
and appearance," expressed his utter surprise to learn that
they had yellow skins. The shift of opinion from relative in-
difference and casual condescension toward unbending hos-

tility in the early nineteenth century can be seen in the young Ralph Waldo Emerson's denunciation of China as "that booby nation" of "venerable vegetation . . . [and] reverend dullness." The "hoary ideot" China "preserved to a hair for 3 or 4,000 years the ugliest features in the world" and could say to "the convocation of nations," before which even the African could boast, "I have hewn the wood and drawn the water," only that "I have made the tea." A western judge made the point even more explicitly. In the California case of the *People* versus *Hall* in 1854, the court faced the knotty problem of how to avoid convicting a white man of murder by refusing to hear Chinese witnesses. Since the establishment of white supremacy values in the seventeenth century, the testimony of "Negroes, mulattos, and Indians" against white persons had been rejected or restricted. California followed the same racist laws and practices, and in the Hall case an ingenious California judge found popular favor by deciding that under existing law the Chinese were actually Indians. After all, Columbus thought that he had reached the Sea of China, the Indians originally came from Asia, and the intent of the law was to separate whites from all nonwhites. Certainly Americans found repulsive "the anomalous spectacle of a distinct people . . . whose mendacity is proverbial . . . differing in language, opinions, color, and physical conformation . . . not only [claiming] the right to swear away the life of a citizen but the further privilege of participating with us in administering the affairs of our government."[4]

The anti-Chinese mania which swept California as early as the 1840s has been carelessly (to say the least) attributed to the first few thousand migrants, but the unprecedented and seemingly inexplicable federal ban on Chinese immigration in 1882 cannot be ascribed to Chinese entry into other parts of the country. Nearly all accounts dismiss the initial outburst of California Sinophobia as the incidental result of a largely fortuitous set of circumstances: rowdy southern migrants to the mining camps, the lack of social structure or a core of "respectable" citizens, the silence of the well-meaning majority, and, above all, the intense rivalry of closely divided political factions and parties. Unfortunately, these rationalizations not only fail to explain West Coast events but also lead us farther away from an adequate account of the national events behind the exclusion act. Scholars have generally followed one of two theories: the bill sprang from an alliance of southern Negrophobia and "the California disease," or closely divided national political parties representing a populace largely indifferent to the issues of Chinese immigration made a concession to California Sinophobes. In the final analysis neither theory works because the mystery springs from the unwillingness of historians to acknowledge the long history, the pervasiveness, and the institutionalized nature of white supremacy attitudes and actions. The real (white) American had always been prepared to act toward "intruding" nonwhites with hostility. Thus, long before the arrival of the first Chinese immigrants the old colonial encounter with red and black had structured the basic responses of the dominant white culture.[5]

Since racist responses are older than the Republic itself, one may reasonably ask if the white man really belongs to the New World experience or if he arrived aboard the Mayflower. In fact Elizabethan concepts of beauty stressed North European features, and Englishmen harbored hostile notions about the "savages" and "heathen" of Africa and America, but these opinions seem less central and functional than ideas about more closely watched distinctions such as rich and poor, highborn and lowborn, Anglican and dissenter, English in contrast to Irish, Scottish, or Welsh, and English rather than French or Spanish. (Although the Englishman at home in future generations came to celebrate the virtues of "white civilization" almost as passionately as the American, that chronicle is beyond the scope of this essay.) Thus, the emergence of red, white, and black cannot be explained solely, or even largely, in terms of English precedents.[6]

The potent color distinctions of the colonial period were affected by the American Revolution, but in rather curious ways. The success which meant greater security for many white citizens made the status of red and black even more precarious. (Crispus Attucks, the runaway slave of black-Indian descent who became "the first martyr of the Revolution," provides a very ambiguous symbol.) Although the revolutionary struggle gave some impetus to the fragile antislavery forces, the old British government had less enthusiasm for slavery and the rapid dispossession of western Indians than the new nation. Moreover, independence immediately made southern slave property more secure. If "a decent respect for the opinions of mankind," or at least those parts of it which were supposed to count, kept the word *white* out of both the Declaration of Independence and the federal Constitution, the fact remains that the new social order clearly did not include blacks and Indians. Much has been made of Jefferson's "deleted clause" against the slave trade, but this proposed sentence in the Declaration was drafted in an implausible effort to make England the scapegoat for American participation in the international slave trade. Certainly Jefferson (like most of his colleagues about whom we know enough to judge) never intended that blacks should be a part of the body politic in white America.

The case of Jefferson reminds us that most presentations about the past are mythological, and none more so than those which deal with race and attempt to make devoted equalitarians of men such as Jefferson and Lincoln. The Lincoln who told "darky" dialect stories, accepted the concept of black racial inferiority, and wished to transport blacks out of the country is set aside in favor of Lincoln the great equalitarian and emancipator. Jefferson's criticisms of slavery have been frequently quoted in such a way as to leave the reader in ignorance of the fact that the Virginian was most concerned about the damage done to the master by the institution of slavery. Quotations on the certainty of future freedom for the blacks are not related to Jefferson's lifelong conviction that emancipated slaves should be sent out of the country. Moreover, Jefferson's mostly private criticisms of slavery were representative of only a small educated elite, and Jefferson in the White House presided over the greatest expansion of slavery in American history. Clearly, the generation which made the Revolution and the new nation paid its respects to white supremacy.[7]

The worst had already been done to the black man, but Indians had even less cause than blacks to rejoice over the birth of a new nation destined to advance relentlessly from the Appalachian Mountains to the Pacific Ocean, killing and dispossessing the red man as an obstacle to "the course of civilization" and America's "manifest destiny." The Declaration of Independence made it clear that "the merciless Indian savage" who conspired with George III in "domestic insurrections" was no part of the new republic. The United States Constitution in the enumeration of congressional powers left the status of Indians extremely ambiguous by speaking of commerce "with foreign nations, and among the several states and with the Indian tribes." The treaty-making process treated Indians as foreign nations and the very first Congress, president, and commissioner of Indian affairs (Secretary of War Henry Knox) all began with the announcement of their intention to grant Indians the conventional rights of foreign peoples. Secretary Knox's assertions that Indian lands "cannot be taken from them unless by their free consent or by right of conquest in case of a just war" and that Indians "ought to be [note the choice of words] considered as foreign nations, not as subjects of any particular state" did not in fact guide Knox or any other major official in Indian policy. The act of Congress (one of the first passed) to which Knox was responding is worth quoting: "The utmost good faith shall always be observed towards the Indians; their land and property shall never be taken from them without their consent; and in their property, rights, and liberty, they shall never be invaded or disturbed, unless in just and lawful wars." As Congress and Secretary Knox may have foreseen, "ought" is not a very binding word, "consent" might be gained by fraud, intimidation, or force, and all acts undertaken by whites turned out to be "just and lawful."[8]

Knox did, in commenting upon the native peoples already extinct, regret the fact that "if the same causes continue the same effects will happen" to other Indian cultures. More candid and explicit was the toast in the officer's mess of the 1779 force sent to burn Iroquois villages in upstate New York: "Civilization or death to all American savages." (For "civilization" substitute "complete subordination to the master race.") Even in times of peace the frontiersman and his sympathizers agreed with the officers of 1779. Hugh Henry Brackenridge referred to the red men as "the animals vulgarly called Indians" and described their most useful function as providing fertilizer: "The Indians' bones must enrich the soil before the plough of civilized man can open it." The Jacksonians resorted to this kind of violent rhetoric even more frequently. President Jackson himself privately abused the red man in the most extreme language, and in public messages phrased the fundamental question in this way: "What *good man* [italics added] would prefer a country covered with forests and ranged by a few thousand savages to our extensive Republic, studded with cities, towns, and prosperous farms . . . occupied by more than 12,000,000 people and filled with all the blessings of liberty, civilization, and religion." Seemingly, all the forces of good and religion would laud the white man who dispatched the "squalid savages" as quickly as possible.

Thomas Hart Benton, like many of his contemporaries, drew a moral for the world from white-Indian relations in America: "The white race alone received the divine command to subdue and replenish the earth . . . [and] civilization or extinction has been the fate of all people who have found themselves to be in the path of advancing whites." Red and black men, presumably, should have been grateful for the option of mass destruction or total subordination to white "civilization." An ordinary Ohio farmer, when asked if a wretched handful of surviving Miamis ever caused any trouble, replied, "No . . . if any . . . displease us, we take them out of doors and kick them a little, for they are like dogs, and will love you better for it."[9]

Quite another Indian, the noble and virtuous savage, served as a foil to the corrupt and decadent "civilized" man in the many thousands of pages devoted to this theme and invaded the minds of men and women remote from public policy, the frontier, and the battlefield. The Kansas senator who measured sympathy for the Indian by the amount of distance between the white sympathizer and the "noble redskin" had a point. The defender of the Indian seldom got near the object of his concern, and the actual history of the red man centered around the violence and aggression inflicted on him by the constantly encroaching whites. Writers, artists, and publicists often seemed merely to be specializing in a different kind of exploitation—one which was intellectual rather than economic or political.

Even in politics the self-appointed friend of the Indian generally turned out to be destructive, and the depredations of white power can be seen more effectively in the allegedly sympathetic Franklins and Jeffersons than in the overtly hostile Brackenridges and Jacksons. Franklin certainly expressed sympathy toward the native American on many occasions, and wrote the often quoted indictment of the Paxton boys who massacred men, women, and children from the small remnants of a defeated and peaceful Indian tribe. In several essays and letters Franklin even made an effort to imagine himself as an Indian, but he also discussed in a matter-of-fact manner the doom which he anticipated for the native American. With a humor which might escape the victim he described rum as "the appointed means" of fulfilling "the design of Providence to extirpate these savages in order to make room for the cultivators of the earth." As one might expect, he assumed that the continent belonged to the white man and modestly advanced this goal more than once.[10]

If the Indian had a "best friend" among the whites it was Thomas Jefferson, who repeatedly exempted the native American from the gross inferiority which he attributed to the black man. Jefferson returned again and again throughout his long life to the theme of Indian virtues—intellect, imagination, fortitude, courage, great capacity for human growth, and a "sublime oratory" comparable to the best of Demosthenes and Cicero. Yet, quite another Jeffersonian point of view lurks in the vast corpus of his letters and papers. The accusation in the Declaration of Independence has already been noted, and later in the same year when Indian warfare threatened his home country, he insisted that "nothing will reduce those wretches so soon as pushing the war into the heart of their country. But I would not stop there. I would never cease pursuing them while one of them remained on this side of the Mississippi. . . . [They] are a useless, expensive, and ungovernable ally." A few years later in a sharp reversal of opinion Jefferson proved himself the poorest of prophets. "It may be regarded as certain that not a foot of land will ever be taken from the Indians, without their own consent. The sacredness of their rights is felt by all thinking persons in America."

Yet Jefferson himself did more than almost any other chief executive to plunder the Indian by presiding over the seizure of one hundred million acres of land through "persuasion," intimidation, bribery, and hastily devised and seldom honored treaties often forced upon both authentic and self-appointed chiefs, who failed to understand the white man's concept of property and who lacked the authority to surrender the tribal heritage. Jefferson repeatedly expressed the belief that the Indians would continue to be crushed as long as they caused trouble for the inevitably dominant whites. The major hope for the red man, it seemed, lay in retreating to lands west of the Mississippi which the whites did not want. All of this was said and done by a president who lived in a kind of fantasy land inhabited by highly favorable reports about the growing friendship of whites and Indians. In 1803 he promised "to live in perpetual peace with the Indians, to cultivate an affectionate attachment . . . by everything just and liberal." The gap between rhetoric and action is truly astonishing, and sometimes Jefferson simply brushed aside the rhetoric. In 1812 he noted that the "backward" Indian would be thrust into new retreats by the whites: "They will relapse into barbarism and misery . . . and we shall be obliged to drive them with the beasts of the forest into the stony [Rocky] mountains." Jefferson's relative lack of bigotry did not mean much to the Indians who suffered the disastrous results of his policies. Moreover, Jefferson thought that the highest praise to be bestowed on those magnificent, courageous, and eloquent people was that with enough high-minded striving and effort they might ultimately hope to cease being Indians and become instead fully assimilated white "sodbusters."[11]

The five "civilized" tribes in the South made an impressive attempt to follow Jefferson's advice. The Cherokees, by conventional American standards, acquired at least as high a level of "civilization" as their white Georgia adversaries, even to the point of acquiring a substantial number of black slaves and a few cotton plantations. Unfortunately, Cherokee newspapers, schools, farms, and skilled trades did not stop the insatiable land-grabbers, President Jackson, and, ultimately, federal troops. John Marshall accepted the Cherokees as a "domestic dependent nation" (a phrase that almost defies rational analysis) with a treaty binding on the United States, but his decision had no force and after the Civil War Congress passed legislation which made it possible to unilaterally "abrogate" Indian treaties. (So much for "domestic dependent nations.") Although the fourteenth amendment accepted the citizenship of "all persons born in the United States," that status was not even abstractly enjoyed by Indians until the 1920s.[12]

Jefferson might praise the noble red man, Jackson might denounce the evil savage, and Lincoln might promise a new order, but the results for the Indian were all the same. Ironically, the Radical Republican era marked the beginning of a new cycle of repression. Still to come were a few more battles, scattered lynchings, unprovoked massacres of men, women, and children at Sand Creek, Wounded Knee, and elsewhere, as well as an incredible amount of private aggression and random violence. But three hundred years of military struggle had nearly come to an end. The old land frauds would continue (by 1934, 86 million acres were gone, the best of 138 million left after the Indian wars) as wretched and starving bands huddled together in reservations increasingly inadequate for sustaining the old ways. Millions of dollars of Indian funds supported the Office of Indian Affairs while its corrupt agents stole their rations, appropriated their cattle, and robbed them of their lands. The post-1870 era gave birth to a cultural war against the Indians in which the United States government launched systematic assaults on Indian religions, languages, and customs. Boarding schools were established which taught English as well as shame to the possessors of "the barbarous dialects." Agents and teachers ridiculed the ancient ways, forbade the children to practice the old rituals, and cut their students' hair—sometimes at gunpoint. Usually federal employees were assisted by hordes of aggressively competitive Baptist, Methodist, Mormon, and Catholic missionaries.

The Dawes Act, aimed at forcing Indians to divide communal lands into individual plots, was to be the final solution to the Indian problem. By division and purchase the federal government recovered 17 million acres in 1890 alone, but the private land-grabbers got a still larger quantity from the five civilized tribes. Physical force, squatting, corrupt contracts, and myriad forms of deception all brought millions of acres into white hands, and when new legislation made outright purchase difficult, leasing became the new vehicle of fraud. Among the weapons for squeezing profits from leasing were excessive fees, illegal mortgages and liens, forged wills, and the "guardianship of minors and incompetent Indians."

Despite all that the white man did, the often demoralized and half-starved red man continued to share his food, support his old people, and cling to other members of his tribe. In brief he cherished his ancient original sin of preferring communal life to private property, possessive individualism, and competitive life-styles. Almost inevitably there were some ultra-Americans in the 1920s who denounced the Indians and their supporters as Communists and possibly agents of Moscow. Thus the oldest Americanism became the newest subversion.[13]

To consider the black man as well as the Indian is to become aware of still more historical ironies. The enslaved African paid an extraordinarily high blood price to the imperialist who often credited the *defeated* Indian with many virtues in a comparative rhetorical context which stripped the black man of the last vestiges of humanity. For example, it is worth noting that in the sixteenth century the Spanish priest Bartalome de Las Casas advocated for "humanitarian" reasons the enslavement of Africans to replace the perishing Indians as forced laborers. In United States history the expansion of American democracy often meant the advance of white racism; and the conquest and removal of Indians made it possible for whites to find admirable qualities in the defeated braves which the African allegedly lacked. Indians were probably more feared and hated on a precarious frontier during a period of active warfare, but as the frontier moved west and most eastern Indians were exterminated or forced across the Mississippi, hatred of the red man diminished sharply. A more pervasive and massive white hostility toward blacks existed even in the absence of danger and, indeed, infected areas which were entirely or nearly devoid of black inhabitants. The fact that about fifty scattered black persons lived in Oregon during the 1850s and had never been seen by most whites did not prevent the territorial legislature from expressing a rabid Negrophobia.[14]

Why were the hatred and contempt more pervasive and enduring toward the black man? Sheer numbers provide a part of the answer. Long before the end of the colonial period blacks greatly exceeded the diminishing and retreating Indian population. The white man wanted land from the Indians and labor from the black people, therefore he had to accept the blacks as a permanent if despised group with whom he had to deal every day. In a sense the whites hated the blacks *because* they wanted and needed their labor so much. Moreover, it was impossible to ignore the continuing presence of the black man in the life of the nation in patterns of work and play, songs and stereotypes, and guilt and apprehensions. The defeated and largely displaced Indian could be thrust aside and "forgiven," but the preservation of dominant myths of liberty, equality, and American innocence demanded much more strongly the continuing dehumanization of the black man. Americans could not forget the long centuries of war with the Indians for the land, and though the Indian had to bear the reputation of a barbarian stripped of land he did not merit, few Americans wished to denigrate (literally to reduce to "nigger" status) completely an old and persistent foe for fear of making their own fighting prowess inconsequential and their final victory unworthy. White America needed to remember Indian courage and to forget black resistance. It was less disturbing to think of Tecumseh than of Nat Turner, and it was best to forget that most Africans had been wrenched from their homelands in small groups and denied the historical experience of the Indians who struggled on native soil for the existence of their land and people.

That a larger number of blacks than Indians survived the initial introduction to plantation slavery was regarded by the whites not as possible evidence of black social strength, but as positive proof of greater stupidity, cowardice, and a natural aptitude for slavery. Moreover when the existence of rebels such as Nat Turner could not be denied, their rebellions were described as "senseless violence." In other cases the historians and the mythicizers conveniently forgot that resistance and rebellion had taken place. The Seminole Wars of the 1830s and 1840s, which might well be called the Seminole-Negro Wars, constituted the longest, bloodiest, and most expensive Indian wars the United States ever fought. From the earliest days the southern frontier feared the specter of black-red cooperation. It is interesting to note that the Florida wars provide one of the best instances of persistent black resistance. When peace came to Florida, some blacks and Indian allies moved to northern Mexico where they waged guerilla warfare for years against Texas planters who were so skeptical about black courage that they invented fanciful stories about refugee Mameluke soldiers from the remote Ottoman Empire to explain the presence of the troublesome darkskinned fighters.[15]

Of white imperiousness and white contacts with red and black we know much, but of initial contacts between African and Indian we know very little. In the Southeast, the Chickasaws, Choctaws, Cherokees, and Creeks (in that order) adopted some white attitudes toward blacks, but a few Cherokees, some Creeks, and a goodly number of Seminoles married blacks and worked and fought together with them in substantial numbers. The Seminoles, in particular, took a sympathetic stance. In the end, however, whites subordinated both black and red to their caste system. The long-range effect of white supremacy was to compel most southern Indian tribes to accept white dominion and to seek gratification in a sense of superiority to the blacks. In the minds of most whites the situation was quite simple—the red man had been banished to the far West or limited to a few unimportant eastern conclaves, and where white, red, and black happened to live in physical proximity, a triple caste system existed with blacks at the bottom. Yet actual social situations contained many incongruities which official ideology did not allow for. Although whites almost always granted the superiority of Indians to blacks, they frequently attempted to force Indian children into black schools. In Mississippi at the turn of the twentieth century consciousness of status and color was so intense that in several parts of the state the ruling elite maintained four separate school systems for whites, blacks, Indians, and recent immigrants from southern Italy. If some Indians learned condescension from whites, so did some blacks: Western Indians who attended Hampton Institute after the Civil War and lived in the Indian dormitory suffered from the stigma of being considered savages, and the black "buffalo" soldiers who fought in Indian wars toward the end of the nineteenth century often spoke scornfully of their red adversaries.[16]

It is worth remembering that in many instances "red," "white," and "black" as monolithic entities rest on fantasies. In colonial sources hundreds of largely ignored records and papers refer to half-breeds, mulattoes, mustees, mestizos, mistizos, 'French" Indians, and "Spanish" Indians. We must remember the harshness of white servitude in the seventeenth century, the existence of Indian slavery in many English colonies, and the common meeting grounds explored by different types of victims. We have been taught to ignore Indian slavery (much research needs to be done here) and to let the subject pass with a few brief remarks, but colonial whites frequently showed a willingness to enslave the native Americans as well as the blacks. Nearly all the colonies at the time of the Revolution had a few Indian slaves; Missouri had several as late as the 1830s; and the dockets of many Southern courts in the 1820s and 1830s contained cases of slaves trying to gain their freedom on the ground that they were the illegally enslaved children of free Indian women. Indian slavery did not become clearly illegal until the thirteenth amendment and by that time many decimated eastern tribes (forbidden by law to marry whites) had lost their identity among a much larger number of black people.

Despite much group hostility a significant number of liaisons existed among whites and blacks, whites and Indians, and Indians and blacks. The offspring of these illegitimate unions sometimes entered social groups from which they were excluded by the official definitions of the social system. Some whites "went Indian"; hundreds of thousands of people with both European and African ancestors ended by passing as white; many persons of largely African ancestry accepted an Indian identity; and some individuals with largely European or Indian forebears became "black." We can learn something about color attitudes in a few persistent tri-ethnic communities of men and women with varying degrees of Indian, black, and European ancestors. Faced with the reality of white domination and rejection, these people of multiple origins tried, often successfully, to maintain a separate identity as well as a social status superior to that of the blacks. In recent years at least a few of these communities have disintegrated. Most of them exist at a level of poverty below that of the black majority, and black communities have become the most dynamic sources of social change among minority groups.

The existence of American tri-ethnic communities sprang from the determination of whites to continue the debasement of blacks, as well as from the desperate striving of mixed communities to avoid at all costs the despised label of "Negro." It is interesting to note that the Indians of Lumberton, North Carolina, became "Croatans" by act of the North Carolina legislature in 1885. The white legislators, persuaded that the Lumberton Indians sprang from settlers of "the lost colony" and the native people the colonists had married, prohibited intermarriage with Negroes to avoid "debasing white blood" any further! Usually, however, whites gave little thought to the few remnants of the eastern Indians.

Presumably an iron wall of total separation existed between white and black, and whites almost invariably tried to deny the obvious evidence of their senses by acting as if Americans came in only one of two totally opposite and different colors. (The inevitable confusion appeared, among other places and times, during the suppression of the Philippine insurrection when white soldiers commonly spoke of Filipinos as "niggers." Yet the same soldiers back in America would almost certainly have made careful distinctions between "Indians" and "Negroes.") When legislators tried to work with the problem, they sometimes said that a Negro was a person with one-quarter, one-eighth, one-sixteenth, one-thirty-second, or "any known trace" of African ancestry. White public opinion also granted the all-conquering nature of "Negro blood," often to the extent of asserting that "one drop" would overwhelm gallons of "European blood." Every village and county which contained both peoples had its secrets of black-white kinships, but whites continued to stress the terrible black "biological threat" to the white race. According to common assertion "race-mixing" and "mongrelization of the races," seemingly a truly monstrous fate, had never happened and should be prevented at any cost.

Yet in conduct and speech whites frequently contradicted their own passionately expounded rhetoric. For example, the fact of race mixture was often acknowledged to demonstrate that any merit or ability displayed by a black person could be attributed to white ancestry. Before the Civil War many planters emancipated those slaves closest to their own color, and a much more common means of expressing color preference was to allow light-skinned slaves to escape the brutal conditions of field labor by becoming house servants. After Civil War and Reconstruction access to better occupations such as barbering, farming, catering, and the skilled trades was given much more freely to black persons of mixed ancestry. Moreover, these economic patterns were reinforced in countless ways by a culture which made black synonymous with sin, dishonesty, death, treachery, and ugliness and associated white with God, heaven, angels, virtue, purity, morality, and beauty. Nevertheless the prosperous black who traded on a lighter skin color to the extent of forgetting his membership in a subordinate caste courted death. Favors promised by the white man to the more industrious and the less offensive often turned out to be the promises of, as the expression goes, Indian givers. White Americans insisted both on keeping blacks in the one rank assigned to all persons with known African ancestors, and at the same time they acted in complete contradiction to this principle by making a number of color distinctions in daily life.

Most status groups in the dominant caste supported capitalism and white supremacy and sought simultaneously both "equality" and higher status in ways which made white racism more functional. Perhaps it will be best to clarify the point by making more explicit the nature of the clash between official ideology and conflicting social experiences. White Americans could have their cake and eat it too by preaching universal equality while simultaneously reaping status gains from the maintenance of servile castes. The American creed of "equality of opportunity" often seemed a mere euphemism for the frantic scramble for wealth, status, and power in which a few would gain a great deal of "equality," or to speak more plainly, ascendancy over others. These basic contradictions have made realistic assessments of American society hard to come by. Americans, seeing themselves as an innocent people, found it difficult to acknowledge that the continent was gained by the near extermination of the Indian, the exploitation of poor whites and immigrants, and the oppression of black people. Because America is by definition the land of freedom and equality, the elaborate system of status and caste as well as the long history of imperialism and racial oppression must be denied. Recently, however, the emergence of oppressed minorities, particularly blacks, has pushed the nation toward a confrontation with its own history which must end in a restructuring of American society or in massive civil strife.

In the final analysis American history is a part of Western history, and racism must be traced to its European roots. The United States did develop a more fanatical domestic version of white supremacy, but American racism can best be seen in the context of world history. For generations "civilized"

Europeans expressed irritation over white American arrogance toward the black middle class: in 1850 Frederick Douglass could hope to gain the sympathetic ear of English aristocrats over indignities he suffered after his flight from slavery; in 1918 French army officers could express disgust over the determination of white Americans to treat black officers as subhuman; Richard Wright could realistically hope to find a life largely free of harassment by fleeing to Paris in 1945; and even today black Mississippians can evoke concerned responses among millions of Europeans. Protestations of European "innocence," however, bear a strong resemblance to similar myths about innocent Americans. In the early years of the twentieth century it would have been easy to raise money for American lynch victims in Brussels but very difficult to get a hearing over the massacre of hundreds of thousands of people in the Belgian Congo. For centuries white European imperialists sacked the world and prospered at the expense of "the lesser breeds without." For many generations France, England, and other Western nations espoused domestic equality and liberty, while the very same nations escalated the colonial oppression of the Afro-Asian and Latin American peoples of the world.

To make the circle complete, the United States has become the neocolonial heir to European world power in our own time. It was more than an interesting curiosity during the 1960s when United States troops in Vietnam began to refer to areas partly under the control of the National Liberation Front as "Indian country." Perhaps a closer study of the history of red, white, and black will help to point the way toward solutions for the internal and external contradictions with which this society is grappling.

NOTES

1. Jean-Paul Sartre, "Portrait of the Anti-Semite," *Partisan Review* 13 (1946): 163–178, and Sartre's preface to Frantz Fanon, *The Wretched of the Earth*, trans. Constance Farrington (London: McGibbon and Kee, 1965), pp. 26–84. On American Indians and blacks see Charles M. Hudson, ed., *Red, White, and Black: Symposium on Indians in the Old South* (Athens: University of Georgia Press, 1971).

2. On black nationalism see Edwin S. Redkey, *Black Exodus, 1890–1910*

(New Haven, Conn.: Yale University Press, 1969); John Bracey, Jr. et al., eds., *Black Nationalism in America* (Indianapolis: Bobbs-Merrill, 1970); and Raymond F. Betts, ed., *The Ideology of Blackness* (Lexington, Mass.: D. C. Heath, 1971).

3. Franklin in Leonard Labaree et al., *The Papers of Benjamin Franklin*, 15 vols. to date (New Haven, Conn.: Yale University Press, 1959–), 4: 225–234. On color symbolism see Arrah B. Evarts, "Color Symbolism," *Psychoanalytic Review* 6 (1919): 129–134, and the extensive notes and bibliography in Harold B. Isaacs, *The New World of Negro Americans* (New York: John Day, 1963).

4. For the Hall case see Helen Catterall, *Judicial Cases Concerning Slavery*, 5 vols. (Washington, D.C.: Government Printing Office, 1926–1937), 5: 252–253. See also William H. Gillman et al., eds., *The Journals and Miscellaneous Notebooks of Ralph Waldo Emerson*, 8 vols. to date (Cambridge, Mass.: Harvard University Press, 1967–), 6: 224, and John C. Fitzpatrick, ed., *The Writings of George Washington*, 39 vols. (Washington, D.C.: Government Printing Office, 1931–1944), 6: 239.

5. The older and more conventional accounts of the Chinese are in Mary Coolidge, *Chinese Immigration* (New York: Henry Holt, 1909), Elmer Sandmeyer, *The Anti-Chinese Movement in California* (Urbana: University of Illinois Press, 1938), and John Higham, *Strangers in the Land* (New Brunswick, N.J.: Rutgers University Press, 1963). The leading revisionist works are Gunther Barth, *Bitter Strength* (Cambridge, Mass.: Harvard University Press, 1964), Stuart C. Miller, *The Unwelcome Immigrant* (Berkeley: University of California Press, 1969), and Robert F. Heizer and Alan J. Almquist, *The Other Californians: Prejudice and Discrimination under Spain, Mexico, and the U.S. to 1920* (Berkeley: University of California Press, 1971).

6. See Winthrop D. Jordan, *White over Black* (Chapel Hill: University of North Carolina Press, 1968), especially chap. 2, and Phillip D. Curtain, *The Image of Africa* (Madison: University of Wisconsin Press, 1967).

7. On Jefferson see Robert M. McColley, *Slavery in Jeffersonian Virginia* (Urbana: University of Illinois Press, 1964). See also Gary B. Nash and Richard Weiss, *The Great Fear* (New York: Holt, Rinehart and Winston, 1970), especially pp. 1–27, 71–79. On black and red status see Lorenzo J. Greene, *The Negro in Colonial New England* (New York: Columbia University Press, 1942). On Lincoln see the text and notes in Charles Crowe, *The Age of Civil War and Reconstruction* (Homewood, Ill.: Dorsey Press, 1966), pp. 239–257.

8. For the Knox quotations see *American State Papers*, United States Congress, 1789–1838, Indian Affairs, 57 vols. (Washington, D.C.: Gales and Seaton, 1832–1861), 1: 53. See also *A Sketch of the Development of the Bureau of Indian Affairs* (Washington, D.C.: Government Printing Office, 1956), pp. 1–3, and Roy H. Pearce, *The Savages of America* (Baltimore, Md.: Johns Hopkins University Press, 1953), chap. 1. More information on Knox can be found in Alvin M. Josephy, Jr., *The Indian Heritage of America* (New York: Bantam, 1968), p. 315, and Jack D. Forbes, *The Indian in America's Past* (Englewood Cliffs, N.J.: Prentice-Hall, 1964), p. 98.

9. For the quotations and opinions of Brackenridge, Jackson, Benton, and others see Wilcomb E. Washburn, "The Moral and Legal Justification for Dispossessing the Indian," in *Seventeenth-Century America*, James M.

Smith, ed. (Chapel Hill: University of North Carolina Press, 1959), pp. 18–34; Vine Deloria, Jr., *Custer Died For Your Sins* (New York: Avon, 1970), pp. 35–60; Alice Marriot and Carol K. Rachlin, *American Epic: The Story of the American Indian* (New York: Putnam's, 1969), pp. 116, 130, 163, 172; and Forbes, *The Indian in America's Past*, pp. 98–112.

10. *The Autobiography of Benjamin Franklin*, Max Farrand, ed. (Berkeley: University of California Press, 1949), p. 149.

11. The Jefferson quotations are from John P. Foley, *The Jefferson Cyclopedia* (New York: Funk and Wagnalls, 1900), pp. 420–423.

12. See Mary E. Young, *Redskins, Ruffleshirts and Rednecks: Indian Allotments in Alabama and Mississippi* (Norman: University of Oklahoma Press, 1961); Albert K. Weinberg, *Manifest Destiny* (Baltimore, Md., Johns Hopkins University Press, 1935); and William T. Hagan, *American Indians* (Chicago: University of Chicago Press, 1961).

13. See Hagan, *American Indians*, and Edward H. Spicer, *A Short History of the Indians of the U.S.* (New York: Anvil, 1969). Two good anthologies are Wilcomb E. Washburn, *The Indian and the White Man* (Garden City, N.Y.: Anchor, 1964) and Jack D. Forbes, *The Indian in America's Past* (Englewood Cliffs, N.J.: Prentice-Hall, 1964). See also Vine Deloria, Jr., *Of Utmost Good Faith* (New York: Bantam, 1972).

14. On Negrophobia see Forrest G. Wood, *Black Scare: Racist Response to Emancipation and Reconstruction* (Berkeley: University of California Press, 1968), and Leon Litwack, *North of Slavery* (Chicago: University of Chicago Press, 1961). Many black responses are recorded in Herbert Aptheker, *A Documentary History of the Negro People in the U.S.* (New York: Associated Publishers, 1951).

15. See Laurence Foster, *Negroes and Indians in the Southeast* (Washington, D.C.: Association for the Study of Negro Life and History, 1928). Kenneth W. Porter has written many articles about blacks and Indians in the *Journal of Negro History* and elsewhere. Herbert Aptheker has stressed black resistance but also provides information about Indian and black-Indian struggles; in particular see his *American Negro Slave Revolts* (New York: Columbia University Press, 1943). Carter G. Woodson and several other scholars have written notable essays for the *Journal of Negro History*. On the frontier and Mexico see Kenneth W. Porter, "Negroes and Indians on the Texas Frontier, 1831–1876," *Journal of Negro History* 41 (1956): 152–170, and Ralph A. Smith, "The Mamelukes of West Texas and Mexico," *West Texas History Yearbook* 4 (1963): 5–22.

16. On the "buffalo soldiers" see Willard B. Gatewood, ed., *Smoked Yankees and the Struggle for Empire* (Urbana: University of Illinois Press, 1972).

SOURCES CITED

Aptheker, Herbert. *A Documentary History of the Negro People in the U. S.* New York: Associated Publishers, 1951.

Aptheker, Herbert. *American Negro Slave Revolts.* New York: Columbia University Press, 1943.

Barth, Gunther. *Bitter Strength.* Cambridge, Mass.: Harvard University Press, 1964.

Betts, Raymond F., ed. *The Ideology of Blackness*. Lexington, Mass.: D. C. Heath, 1971.

Bracey, John, Jr., et al., eds. *Black Nationalism in America*. Indianapolis: Bobbs-Merrill, 1970.

Catterall, Helen. *Judicial Cases Concerning Slavery*. Vol. 5. Washington, D.C.: Government Printing Office, 1926–1937.

Coolidge, Mary. *Chinese Immigration*. New York: Henry Holt, 1909.

Crowe, Charles. *The Age of Civil War and Reconstruction*. Homewood, Ill.: Dorsey Press, 1966.

Curtain, Phillip. *The Image of Africa*. Madison: University of Wisconsin Press, 1967.

Deloria, Vine, Jr. *Custer Died For Your Sins*. New York: Avon, 1970.

Deloria, Vine, Jr. *Of Utmost Good Faith*. New York: Bantam, 1972.

Emerson, Ralph Waldo. *The Journals and Miscellaneous Notebook of Ralph Waldo Emerson*. Edited by William H. Gillman et al. Vol. 6. Cambridge, Mass. Harvard University Press, 1967–.

Evarts, Arrah B. "Color Symbolism." *Psychoanalytic Review* 6 (1919): 129–134.

Fanon, Frantz. *The Wretched of the Earth*. Translated by Constance Farrington. London: McGibbon and Kee, 1965.

Foley, John P. *The Jefferson Cyclopedia*. New York: Funk and Wagnalls, 1900.

Forbes, Jack D. *The Indian in America's Past*. Englewood Cliffs, N.J.: Prentice-Hall, 1964.

Foster, Laurence. *Negroes and Indians in the Southeast*. Washington, D.C.: Association for the Study of Negro Life and History, 1928.

Franklin, Benjamin. *The Autobiography of Benjamin Franklin*. Edited by Max Farrand. Berkeley: University of California Press, 1949.

Franklin, Benjamin. *The Papers of Benjamin Franklin*. Edited by Leonard Labaree et al. Vol. 4. New Haven, Conn.: Yale University Press, 1959–.

Greene, Lorenzo J. *The Negro in Colonial New England*. New York: Columbia University Press, 1942.

Gatewood, Willard B., ed. *Smoked Yankees and the Struggle for Empire*. Urbana: University of Illinois Press, 1972.

Hagan, William T. *American Indians*. Chicago: University of Chicago Press, 1961.

Heizer, Robert F., and Almquist, Alan J. *The Other Californians: Prejudice and Discrimination under Spain, Mexico, and the U. S. to 1920*. Berkeley: University of California, 1971.

Higham, John. *Strangers in the Land*. New Brunswick, N.J.: Rutgers University Press, 1963.

Hudson, Charles M., ed. *Red, White, and Black: Symposium on Indians in the Old South*. Athens: University of Georgia Press, 1971.

Isaacs, Harold B. *The New World of Negro Americans*. New York: John Day, 1963.

Jordan, Winthrop D. *White over Black*. Chapel Hill: University of North Carolina Press, 1968.

Josephy, Alvin M., Jr. *The Indian Heritage of America*. New York: Bantam, 1968.

Litwack, Leon. *North of Slavery*. Chicago: University of Chicago Press, 1961.

McColley, Robert M. *Slavery in Jeffersonian Virginia.* Urbana: University of Illinois Press, 1964.

Marriot, Alice, and Rachlin, Carol K. *American Epic: The Story of the American Indian.* New York: Putnam's, 1969.

Miller, Stuart C. *The Unwelcome Immigrant.* Berkeley: University of California Press, 1969.

Nash, Gary B., and Weiss, Richard. *The Great Fear.* New York: Holt, Rinehart and Winston, 1970.

Pearce, Roy H. *The Savages of America.* Baltimore, Md.: Johns Hopkins University Press, 1953.

Porter, Kenneth W. "Negroes and Indians on the Texas Frontier, 1831–1876." *Journal of Negro History* 41 (1956): 152–170.

Redkey, Edwin S. *Black Exodus, 1890–1910.* New Haven, Conn.: Yale University Press, 1969.

Sandmeyer, Elmer. *The Anti-Chinese Movement in California.* Urbana: University of Illinois Press, 1938.

Sartre, Jean-Paul. "Portrait of the Anti-Semite." *Partisan Review* 13 (1946): 163–178.

Smith, Ralph A. "The Mamelukes of West Texas and Mexico," *West Texas History Yearbook* 4 (1963): 5–22.

Spicer, Edward H., Jr. *A Short History of the Indians of the U.S.* New York: Anvil, 1969.

Washburn, Wilcomb E. *The Indian and the White Man.* Garden City, N.Y.: Anchor, 1964.

Washburn, Wilcomb E. "The Moral and Legal Justification for Dispossessing the Indian." In *Seventeenth-Century America*, edited by James M. Smith. Chapel Hill: University of North Carolina Press, 1959.

Washington, George. *The Writings of George Washington.* Edited by John C. Fitzpatrick. Vol. 6. Washington, D.C.: Government Printing Office, 1931–1944.

Weinberg, Albert K. *Manifest Destiny.* Baltimore, Md.: Johns Hopkins University Press, 1935.

Wood, Forrest G. *Black Scare: Racist Response to Emancipation and Reconstruction.* Berkeley: University of California Press, 1968.

Young, Mary E. *Redskins, Ruffleshirts and Rednecks: Indian Allotments in Alabama and Mississippi.* Norman: University of Oklahoma Press, 1961.

A Late Bibliographical Note

Among the major works relevant to this essay which were not available or had not been published when I completed this essay in 1971 are Wesley Frank Craven, *White, Red, and Black: The Seventeenth Century Virginian* (Charlottesville: University Press of Virginia, 1971); Wilbur Jacobs, *Dispossessing the American Indian: Indians and Whites on the Colonial Frontier* (New York: Scribner's, 1972); Bernard W. Sheehan, *Seeds of Extinction: Jeffersonian Philanthrophy and the American Indian* (Chapel Hill: University of North Carolina Press, 1973); and Wilcomb E. Washburn, *Red Man's Land, White Man's Law: A Study of the Past and Present Status of the American Indian* (New York: Scribner's, 1971). Of special interest is Gary B. Nash's splendid volume, *Red, White, and Black: The Peoples of Early America* (Englewood Cliffs, N.J.: Prentice-Hall, 1974).

C.C.

Contributors

DOUGLAS W. BOYCE is assistant professor of sociology and anthropology at Emory and Henry College in Emory, Virginia. His research interests include eastern North American Indians, ethnohistorical methodology, sociopolitical organization, and ethnic identity. In addition to publishing several essays on the Indians of the Carolinas, he has coauthored an article on the prehistorical and historical demography of the Southeast.

JAMES W. COVINGTON is professor of history and chairman of the senior seminar at the University of Tampa. He is author of *Story of Southeastern Florida*; *Pirates, Indians and Spaniards*; *The British Meet the Seminoles*; *The Third Seminole War* (forthcoming) ; and some fifty articles. His research has been centered mainly with the Utes, Seminoles, Florida history, and the Kennedy Space Center.

CHARLES CROWE is professor of history at the University of Georgia, the author of three books and thirty articles on American intellectual history, utopian socialism, historiography and racial conflict, and a member of the board of editors of the *Journal of Negro History*. He has just completed a manuscript "Racial Violence and Repression in the Progressive Era" and is currently doing research on Indian-black-white relations.

ARTHUR H. DEROSIER, JR., is vice chancellor for academic affairs and professor of history at the University of Mississippi. Though he has published a volume on the Civil War, his major research interest is the removal of the American Indians.

In that field, he has published a volume on the Choctaw removal story plus numerous scholarly articles in leading historical journals on a variety of Indian topics. Currently he is completing a volume on Indian problems since World War II.

RAYMOND D. FOGELSON is associate professor of anthropology in the Department of Anthropology at the University of Chicago. His major research interests include southeastern Indians, ethnology, comparative religion, and psychological anthropology. He has done fieldwork with the Cherokees and with the Shuswaps of British Columbia. He is currently serving as editor of "The Southeast," volume 13 of the new Smithsonian *Handbook of North American Indians.*

JACK D. L. HOLMES, professor of history at the University of Alabama in Birmingham, is editor of the Louisiana Collection Series of Books and Documents on Colonial Louisiana. A specialist in the Spanish borderlands of the Southeast, he is the author of *Gayoso: The Life of a Spanish Governor in the Mississippi Valley* (winner of the 1965 Louisiana Literary Award), *Documentos inéditos para la historia de la Luisiana, 1792–1810,* and *A Guide to Spanish Louisiana, 1762–1806.* He has published articles concerning the Creeks, Seminoles, Choctaws, and Chickasaws in *Die Zinnfigur, Florida Historical Quarterly,* publications of the East and West Tennessee historical societies, and the *Alabama Historical Quarterly.*

CHARLES M. HUDSON is associate professor of anthropology in the Department of Anthropology at the University of Georgia. His main interests are in the Indians of the southeastern United States and in folk belief systems. He is the author of *The Catawba Nation* and editor of *Red, White, and Black: Symposium on Indians in the Old South.*

JAMES H. O'DONNELL III is professor of history at Marietta College, Marietta, Ohio. Author of *The Southern Indians in the American Revolution* (1974), he is presently doing research on a companion piece about the northern Indians. In addition to his interest in the eighteenth-century native American, he is concerned with the problems involved in the historical methodology of native American studies. He is a regular reviewer of books on native American studies for *Choice* and the *Journal of Southern History*.

JOHN H. PETERSON, JR., is associate professor of anthropology at Mississippi State University. In addition to ethnohistory, his major interests are in applied anthropology and minority groups. He has done field research on whites, blacks, and Indians in the Southeast. He is author of a chapter on the Choctaws in volume 13 of the forthcoming Smithsonian *Handbook of North American Indians*. In 1972–1973 he served as chief planner for the Mississippi Band of Choctaws.

ALBERT L. WAHRHAFTIG is assistant professor of anthropology at California State College, Sonoma. He has done field research in Mexico and South America as well as among the Cherokees. He studied the Cherokees as an associate of the Carnegie Corporation Cross-Cultural Education Project of the University of Chicago and is presently engaged in a study of economic development in traditional Cherokee settlements.

Index